PELEG

EARLY EARTH MOVEMENTS

David P. Nelson

PELEGPRESS

Cover; "Atlantic Hemisphere" by H.C.Berann

PELEG
Early Earth Movements
by David P. Nelson

Printed in the United States of America

ISBN 978-0-615-14091-9

www.pelegpress.com

**This book is dedicated to
my loving wife, Gena
and our dear children,**

Gabriel

Joel

Paul

Peter

Rachel

Samuel

Sarah

About the Author

From his youth the author received an excellent understanding of the issues of evolution and historical geology.* With degrees in math and physics, his 20 year professional career was with the aeronautic-space division of Honeywell. It involved inertial systems, gyros, instrumentation, aircraft control and stability phenomena.** His scientific knowledge, background, and love of the Scriptures, inspired insights about the earth. These insights are in this book.

Later in Pittsburgh, he directed the Messianic Jewish Center. Then, in Long Beach, California, he was the pastor of a congregation of Cambodian refugees. He began the Creation Science Fellowship, the organization that sponsors the International Conference on Creationism (ICC). He has referenced two ICC publications in this book.

His respect and defense of the Word are the reasons for this apologetics book.

* His father's pioneering books are reproduced in Volume Five of the Ten Volume Series, **Creationism in Twentieth-Century America, The Creationist Writings of Byron C. Nelson**, Series Editor Ronald L. Numbers, Garland Publishing, Inc., New York & London, 1995.
** At Honeywell the author designed a flight control synthetic rate signal: Patent award 3,171,617, "Control Apparatus for Aircraft. 1965"

CONTENTS

ILLUSTRATIONS

Preface

This book's foundation is the Word of God. My confidence in the Word has come through a long road of tests and trials. The road began with deep trust, and then doubts arose from the claims of literary, historical, and scientific "scholarship." Finally, the Lord brought me back to confidence and trust – it has been a long journey.

In His grace, God has given me a comforting, logical conviction about the Word: God, in love, gave us His Word. He moved on the hearts and minds of His Holy Men, and since that time He has watched over and protected His Word, the Words of His Holy Men, that all His children may have the truth. Because of His protection through these many years, we can trust the Bible. This book is rooted in that truth.

Many folks, untested, have a deep trust in the Bible for which they should be thankful. Knowing the claims of "science" and "scholarship," others are going through tests and trials, struggling to reconcile the Word with those claims. Sadly, some fail and fall away. Knowing these tests, I have written this book to help Believers and those who are tried, who want to know the truth and be in fellowship with God. I have also written this book to advance the science of Historical Geology, a physical witness to the Truth.

The message of this apologetics book, "Early Earth Movements," is an aspect of the Faith. This subject is one small stone in the wall that surrounds and protects the Believer. I do not claim infallibility for this stone. With some of its issues, I have questions for which I wish I knew the answers. Not knowing the answers has not prevented me from pressing on to describe and explain the big picture of earth's early history. I have written this book with the conviction that its thesis is essentially true, and its evidence, descriptions and explanations verify the reliability of Biblical history.

The subject of this book is historical geology. In explaining the geologic evidence of earth's early history, this book will clearly show the harmony of geology with the Word, and that secular historical geology is significantly in error. Furthermore, the geologic evidence abolishes the basic "proof" for Evolution.

Earth's early instabilities are still affecting us. Some ask, "Why do we have earthquakes?" Believers who trust the Lord and His Word have a responsibility to help those who question God when earthquakes, volcanoes, and tsunamis do great damage and destroy so many. Being able to answer those who question God is another reason I have written this book. Apologetics concerning these subjects is important.

Many have encouraged me in writing this book. Some read early drafts and made useful suggestions. Dear ones financed the book and many of the illustrations that Doug Jennings carefully created. Doug also helped in other important ways. For all those that helped I am grateful.

I pray that the Lord will bless the reading and the studying of this book.

Revised, March 2007

David P. Nelson
Clarksburg, West Virginia
www.pelegpress.com

Note: A limited black and white edition of this book was published in the Fall of 2006.

1 - Introduction

We live on a restless earth. Unstable, it shakes here and then there. Its earthquakes are destructive. However, the earth has been more than destroyed here and there. The whole earth was devastated! The rocks record that devastation, destruction beyond our comprehension. Yet, with the eyes of the heart, we can understand that devastation. The Word recorded it. Written for our edification, the Word tells us of that destruction. The Word and the rocks speak to us of the Great Flood of Genesis. Filled with fossils, the remains of life, the rocks reveal God's destruction of that ancient world.

This book will briefly discuss the Flood and that rock record. However, the subject of this book is another earth-encompassing event. That event was not significantly destructive, but it too was global and earth moving. With the eyes of the heart, we can comprehend that event, through the Word and by studying its geologic results.

This book's purpose is to give the evidence and explain why, as the Word declares, the surface of the earth was physically divided. The title of this book, PELEG is from Genesis 10 verse 25. It reads, "One was named Peleg, for during his days the earth was divided." The name, Peleg, is from a Hebrew word meaning "division."

The thesis of this book is that some years after the Flood, the land that had been devastated by the Flood was subjected to forces that divided it. This is an apologetics book.[1] It examines "Plate Tectonics," a development from a recent concept called "Continental Drift." However, contrary to the secular Plate Tectonics theory of the millions-of-years slow separation of all the continents from one landmass, the thesis of this book is that the land division of Peleg's day, the actual beginning of Plate Tectonics, was a recent, moderately gradual, yet powerful event.[2] Furthermore, the division that began in Peleg's time also produced vivid changes to the surface of the earth - our mountain ranges. This book explains these mountain building movements, movements that secular theories fail to explain.

The Bible is historically correct and, where the Bible touches on scientific issues, the Bible has scientific importance. This is especially true concerning historical geology, and specifically the new science of Plate Tectonics. The Bible is relevant concerning geology.

This book is written for those who believe Biblical history. Many Believers maintain that the division spoken of in Genesis 10:25 was a social, or a political, or a spiritual division, a division such as the language division of Babel.[3] Their reservations for believing that Peleg's division was not physical include these reasons: Geologically, that division was too difficult. Geographically, the Bible's description of the earth negates such an event. And chronologically, the Bible does not provide enough time, in the interval between the Flood and Abraham, for global movements of the earth's crust.

However, if in fact a physical division of the earth's surface did occur, then the reservations of these Believers add to the arsenal of weapons used by unbelievers to "prove" that these Believers and their Bible are, "of course," in error. The Bible is vibrant with history, a history that gives light. In the battle between the Light and the Darkness, the Darkness attacks the Bible's history. One purpose of this book is to defeat that damaging weapon of doubt. We can rely on the Bible's history. The purpose of this book is to explain Genesis 10:25 correctly, so that this apologetics book will help Believers defend the Word with solid science and destroy the power of that damaging attack.

The message of this book is that, prior to Peleg, the world endured a universal, catastrophic flood, the great Flood of Genesis. The Flood, its causes and results, created the conditions for the global divisions that followed. However, sequentially, the Flood and the divisions of Peleg were separate events; a significant interval separated them. That is, the explosive phenomena of the Flood with its upheavals had ended and most of its eroding powers and depositions had ceased. Then, after some time, due to ever increasing global instabilities, another awesome event occurred: the separation of the one landmass of the Creation into the continents that we have today. This second moving event began in Peleg's day. Men observed it, and the Word recorded it.

Many subjects are part of this thesis. One important subject, which is not our purpose to pursue, must be addressed. It looms in the background and is destructive to God's salvation plan and to sound science. It is the prevailing "fact of Evolution." Many scientists are doing excellent research and many are producing fine books and media that refute the destructive "fact of Evolution." This book will not examine in depth the issues of Evolution except to declare that almost all evidence supports the Biblical creation account. The following fundamentals are true:

History began with a beautiful - not a "tooth and claw" - creation. However, in God's foreknowledge of Adam and Eve's sin, "The Fall," God designed the creation to bear the Curse He knew He must impose. It was "creation with anticipation." The Curse produced disorder, disease, death and decay. Tooth and claw began. The Curse stained God's beautiful creation. God then allowed the physical Law of the *natural* increase in disorder its full strength and its power began to work. (That Law preceded the Fall.) That Law supports the Biblical history of disorder and decay rather than an evolutionary history of upward progress. That Law negates Evolution.[4]

The Bible's primary purpose is redemption, of undoing all the damage that has been done because of the Fall. One of the damages is death. With the Curse, death entered. However, God will finally destroy the enemy of death and remove the Curse by "...Jesus, whom heaven must receive until the time for restoring all things...." (Acts 3:20-21)

This book is written for the average person, those not trained in physics, mathematics, or geology. Its technical subjects are simplified and yet have been kept accurate. It is written with the conviction that the average person will understand its subjects when read with attention. This book is for those who love the Word and want to know what happened in history in order that they may grow in faith, and when asked, will be able to defend the Faith.

Geologic anomalies and phenomena exist which appear to challenge the thesis of this book. Nevertheless, this book is written with the conviction that almost all evidence supports its thesis. Many "young earth" Creation scientists now believe that the separation of the continents is a well-established fact. They are seeking to understand its geology, its causes, and especially its timing. (Some of these scientists believe that continental separation was part of the Flood event.) This book is written with the hope that it will prompt research based on the thesis that the original landmass began to divide at the time of Peleg, and that some of the forces that created those movements are effective today. Apologetics concerning earth's instabilities, such as earthquakes, is increasingly important.

God has given us the gift of certainty with Biblical history. This certainty is lacking, in various degrees, with all other histories. To establish veracity with other histories, we seek corroborating evidence, the more supporting facts the better. This need certainly applies to historical geology, the primary subject of this book. Therefore, this book also requires supporting facts, geologic data, and reasonable explanations to establish its thesis. This book is written with the conviction that almost all geologic "fingerprints" support its thesis, even to the division itself.

Overview

This book calls the landmass that was divided in the time of Peleg, "Pangaea," the same term that is used in secular geology. Pangaea means "all lands" implying one land. (The Flood came upon this original land.) What was Pangaea and the rest of the earth like? To gain that knowledge, we will briefly analyze our earth's composition and structure in order to put Pangaea's world back together.

The thesis of this book is that some years after the Flood, immense glaciers developed over Northern and Southern Pangaea. (The popular expression for that time is "The Ice Age." Geologists call The Ice Age, "The Glacial Epoch" and "The Pleistocene."[5] We will use the same terminology, without the long-ages time frame.) Those two very large ice masses and their significant lowering of the sea were the factors that fractured and separated Pangaea. Separation probably began at or near the height of the Glacial Epoch.

In order to determine the sequence and the power of that division, we will analyze the veneer of rocks that covers our continents. The deformations of that veneer will help determine when Pangaea's division occurred. Those deformations reveal that tremendous post-Flood forces developed and produced the mountain ranges of today, vivid evidence of the energy and power that divided Pangaea. With that short period of mountain building established, we will show that the secular long-age mountain building theories are inconsistent and do not explain today's mountain ranges.

We will examine how immense those ice masses were. We will analyze the forces and energies those glaciers produced that not only divided Pangaea but also fractured the entire crust under the ocean.[6]

A reasonable question may be, "How could massive glaciers, and their lowering of the sea, produce such profound geologic results?" With respect to an earth that is simply a solid sphere, the two glacial masses and their absorption of water could not have divided Pangaea. However, the area of action concerning Pangaea is the very thin outer layer of the earth. The outer layer, the crust, is proportional to the earth as the thin shell of a hard-boiled egg is to the egg. The earth's outer layer is very thin.[7] Furthermore, the outer layer is mechanically isolated, lubricated, and relatively free from the rest of the earth. Because of its isolation, the forces, stresses and energies that developed in the outer layer were not lost to the earth below, but most accumulated in that outer layer.[8] Thus, with respect to the outer layer, which included Pangaea, the immense glaciers and their prodigious consumption of ocean water were, geologically, very effective. We will show that the "permanent" mass movement of water created inertial forces that were powerful and produced severe geologic changes.

Other important questions will need answers: What was the trigger that caused Pangaea to split? How was it possible to move the new continents that came from Pangaea? Was the adjacent layer below Pangaea and the oceanic crust lubricated enough? Were enough energy and power available to drive the continents apart? We will answer these questions. We will show how the energies that divided Pangaea accumulated to the breaking point.

Having developed answers to these individual issues, we will integrate them into the total picture that produced Pangaea's division and the vivid surface changes and finally, how those stored energies were consumed as the continents moved apart. This summary is called, "Putting the pieces together."

Then we will apply these force and energy phenomena to the two large glaciers that remain to determine the probabilities of earthquakes today. The rise in sea levels from melting Greenland and Antarctica's glaciers and the coastal damage it would cause are long-term concerns. However, our earth is restless today. One purpose of this book is to show that earth's restlessness is an extension of those early earth movements. The book will explain that our earth will continue to be restless, and even more in the future.

Two important proofs are needed: We will examine the geology that shows that the continents of today were once joined, that Pangaea existed and was divided. Then we will examine the evidence revealing the sizes of those two great Pangaean glaciers. In analyzing their locations and motions, especially in the south, the evidence will become very clear that Pangaea divided during the Glacial Epoch.

Finally, what about the issue of time? [9] Was enough time available between the Flood and Abraham to allow for such an incredible global event? We will show that the time-record from the Flood to Abraham (Genesis 11) is not a chronology but a genealogy, that it is not "tight" in terms of time.[10] However, does not radiometric dating, which "proves" that the earth is very old, negate the thesis of this book? We will analyze radiometric dating to show that time need not be a problem concerning Pangaea's division. In analyzing radiometric dating, we will produce a very important by-product: we will destroy the "long-ages" pillar upon which the Theory of Evolution stands.

Concerning the age of the universe, the appendix article, The Stars and Time, analyzes the modern "Big Bang" theory and the stellar evidence.

The appendix has useful subjects. The footnotes add substance to the text.

Chapter 1 Footnotes

1 - "Always be ready to give a defense..." (1 Pet 3:15). The word "defense" (or "answer") is a translation of the Greek word "apologea," from which comes the English word "apologetics." Apologetics is an important aspect of the Faith.

2 - To qualify this assertion concerning Plate Tectonics, see chapter 8, footnote 8.

3 - Socially, God used Babel to separate the people (Gen 11:9). A common interpretation of Gen 10:25 is the following: "[Peleg's division] may refer to the scattering of the descendants of Noah." The Westminster Dictionary of the Bible, Ed. J.D. Davis, The Westminster Press, 1944, 465. Indeed, with that concept in mind, the physical division of the earth advanced the separation of the peoples. "You have fixed all the boundaries of the earth." (Ps 74:17)

4 - This "physical Law" is the 2nd Law of Thermodynamics. For a discussion of this Law and its importance, see the appendix article.

5 - In secular geology the Glacial Epoch is also called the Pleistocene Epoch, and the modern period, which follows the Pleistocene, is called the "Holocene." These two periods together constitute the "Quaternary." This book uses this secular terminology but with a young-earth time frame. The secular theory of a "Paleozoic Glacial Epoch" will be studied in chapter 13, and that time terminology will be explained there. The Pleistocene's secular period is given in chapter 10.

6 - See chapter 8, footnote 8.

7 - To convey their messages, the artists of the cover and of figure 15 amplified the heights of the continents above the ocean floor. On an actual, global scale, the contrasts in elevations between the continents and the ocean floors would be too small to be drawn.

8 - The isolation and lubrication of the thin outer layer of the earth will be described in detail in chapters 8, 9 and 10. However, for preliminary evidence consider the following: If the earth were completely solid, earthquakes could not occur, would not be possible, because independent surface motions would be impossible. Earthquakes occur because the region just below the outer layer of the earth is not solid and rigid but molten and fluid. (Volcanic magmas also reveal this.) "Softness" below the thin outer layer allows the outer layer to move. Thus, earthquakes do occur. This reality is very important concerning the divisions of the earth's surface. The retention and accumulation of stresses and energies in the moveable outer layer ultimately divided Pangaea.

9 - The time-frame of this thesis is "young earth." Several "old earth" theories and stellar phenomena are briefly described and analyzed in Chapter 16 and The Stars and Time article in the appendix.

10 - Though it appears to be "tight," the genealogy of Matthew 1 is also not "tight," i.e. it is not a chronology. See Chapter 17 concerning this significant issue.

2 - Historical Background

Before developing this book's message, it will be profitable to review briefly the history of geologic thought concerning the earth's surface rocks and then the earth's underlying crust.

What is the history of the theories concerning the surface rocks, namely the sedimentary rocks? A coating of sedimentary rocks almost completely covers all continents. Sedimentary rock layers are a thin veneer covering the continents' large core of granite. A common term for these external layers is "strata," an expression frequently used, e.g. the "stratigraphic record." Almost all strata were once sediments, "muds" and debris of various kinds resulting from the erosive power of water or from water-laid chemical deposits. Fossils fill these layers, the evidence of past life.

For several hundred years prior to and into the 19th century, most geologists regarded this stratigraphic record, with its many fossils, as having been catastrophically laid. Many of these geologists believed that these sedimentary rocks resulted from the devastation caused by the Genesis Flood. (Sudden deposition is required to make a fossil, otherwise the dead remains would disappear before being covered.) The technical term used to express this explanation is "catastrophism." Catastrophism was a common theory for the sedimentary rocks, with their fossils, until about 1833, when Charles Lyell popularized the concept of "uniformitarianism."[1] Uniformitarianism advocates that gradual, uniform, geologic processes, operating over long periods, produced the sedimentary layers. Lyell's interpretation led to the expression "the present is the key to the past." According to this theory, the sedimentary layers are, supposedly, a "history book" that records the evolutionary past. (Lyell's theory was very significant. Its long ages provided the time needed by Charles Darwin for his pending [1859] Theory of Evolution.) Since the middle of the 19th century, Lyell's theory has dominated the science of historical geology – until about 1960. The evidences of catastrophe are so pervasive that "neocatastrophism" is now the prevailing secular interpretation of the stratigraphic record.[2]

(The Flood of Genesis explains the stratigraphic fossil record far better than uniformitarian theories. For example, the Flood catastrophe explains the biological "gaps" in the fossil sequences, and the "rapid" extensive extinctions of species. [See "The Crucial Issue" at the end of chapter 5.] Evolution does not adequately explain these phenomena, a significant problem for the Theory. Nevertheless, this partial revival in secular geology toward catastrophism is encouraging.)

Secondly, concerning the earth's crust, what is the history of geologic thought concerning continental drift? (This book uses the expression "continental drift" because of its popular, secular use. Plate Tectonics is now the prevailing theory.) Secular geologists have only recently accepted the phenomena of continental drift. Despite the proposals of several (for example, Alfred Wegener, 1912), almost all secular geologists had firmly rejected continental drift. (For an example of this fact, see "Historical Conflict..." in the appendix.) They believed that the continents were, essentially, permanent. The reason for their rejection was this: what could possibly cause, and enable Pangaea - if it did exist - to separate into the continents of today? They strongly held that conviction, even though geologic and biologic evidences indicated (as Wegener and others demonstrated) that division had indeed occurred.[3]

However, since the 1960's, secular geologists have come to affirm continental drift as a fact and vital to the science of geology. They accepted it, first, because the evidence is overwhelming, and second, they believed they had determined, finally, the mechanism that enabled the continents to move. That mechanism was, supposedly, the slow conveyor-like movements of the mantle under the earth's crust, movements caused by a slow rising and spreading hot mantle upon which the rigid continents and oceanic crust ride. (The mantle lies between the earth's outer surface, the crust, and the earth's core. For more details, see the article, The Earth, in the appendix.) Secular geologists have added to the "drift" theory a process of slow, gravity controlled sinking of the cooler parts of oceanic crust into the hot mantle below, one section pushing itself below an adjacent section, a pulling down process called "subduction." Furthermore, because the evidence indicates that the crust of the earth is divided into separate pieces, called "plates," each plate acting like a raft, the theory of continental drift is now incorporated into the newer discipline called plate tectonics. Secular geology is now integrating the phenomena of plate tectonics into their general theories.

What cataclysmic changes have occurred in secular geologic thinking! [4] Speaking the truth in love, we need to speak a word of criticism: Secular geologists have been grossly wrong. Their errors usually come from a faulty worldview. Even today, their results suffer from denying God's clear revelation of earth's history and of life's history. That is, they base their theories on the foundations of uniformitarianism, long-term neocatastrophism, and on the Theory of Evolution. Therefore, in some of their disciplines, they still do not get the right results. Much of geologic science is very good. Some is not.

Chapter 2 Footnotes

1- Some historians credit James Hutton (1726-1797) and/or John Playfair (1748-1819) with originating the theory of uniformitarianism.

2- Neocatastrophism means "new catastrophism." It is an expression used in secular geology.

3 - In the author's 1947 historical geology class at the University of Wisconsin, continental drift was tersely dismissed.

4 - "How plate tectonics triggered a seismic [intellectual] upheaval in geology." Nature, April 15, 2004, 697.

3 - Pangaea and the Glaciers

Were the division of Pangaea and the movement of the continents possible? Surely, with God all things are possible. Indeed, what caused the prior catastrophe of the Flood? Again, God can do all things. God controls all the forces and phenomena of nature. Concerning the Flood, God "engineered" the forces of the natural world so that they accomplished His purpose. It is beyond our purposes to consider what factors for the Flood God may have used. Nevertheless, the Flood did occur. Not only does the Bible record that history, but also the sedimentary rocks cry out that truth.

Of importance is the fact that the Flood's physical results provided the building blocks for Pangaea's separation. The Biblical account of the Flood, with its geologic and hydrologic factors, indicates the probable post-Flood environment that produced the Glacial Epoch. We will examine that development. Let us return to the opening question, "Were the division of Pangaea and the movement of the continents possible?" To answer that question, we need to determine what Pangaea was like, and then what produced the forces and energies that divided it.

If our continents and oceans came from Pangaea's world, then by examining our earth, we can derive some knowledge of Pangaea's composition, shape, and its oceanic crust. Actually, our knowledge of the structure and composition of our continents, our crusts and our mantle is only partial. We know that oceanic crust is heavier than continental crust but lighter than the mantle. We know that the continents consist primarily of granitic rock, rock formed from the solidification of liquid magmas. (Solidified magmas are called "igneous.") We know that an outer layer of the mantle is "weak," that is, it is plastic and molten. As an isolating layer, this weak layer (called the "asthenosphere") is very important to the thesis of this book. We know that continental crust and oceanic crust (also an igneous rock, primarily basaltic), and a layer at the bottom of the crusts, the "Moho," and the top-most layer of the mantle, are all rigid and even brittle. These three outer layers are bonded together. Called the "lithosphere," these three layers constitute the structure of a plate. See figures 8 and 10. Finally, because the main body of the continents consists of granite, which is a much lighter rock than the mantle, the continents as part of the lithosphere enable the continental-lithosphere plates to float on the weak layer of the underlying mantle.

(For more details concerning the earth's structure and how the earth's characteristics are determined, see the appendix article, "The Earth." An explanation of the use of the word, "crust" is found there.)[1]

The results of putting our continents back together to form Pangaea produce a large landmass. Reconstructions of its dimensions are approximate. See figure 1. (See chapters 12 and 13 to explain Pangaea's northern dimensions – which are not well known.) Clearly, very significant forces were required to divide and separate Pangaea. What were these forces, and how did they develop?

An abundance of geologic evidence reveals that after the Flood, immense glaciers developed on the northern and southern hemispheres of Pangaea. Remains show that these glaciers covered one-third of the earth's land surface, and probably much more.[2]

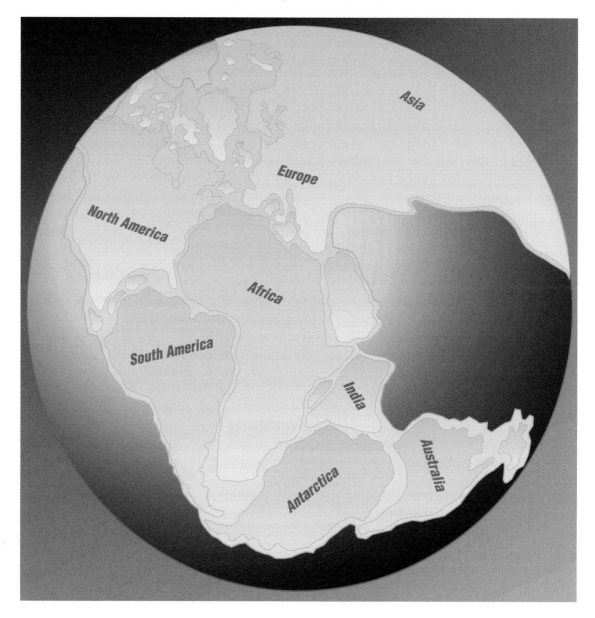

Pangaea: an approximation
Figure 1

This estimate is based on the glacial debris we now have. (Some of the original glaciers were lost into the sea when Pangaea divided, so their glacial remains were also lost.) Putting today's land surfaces back together to form Pangaea, with its glaciers, reveal a heavy, powerful, and effective "dumbbell" arrangement of two very large glacial masses. (See figure 32.)[3] These glaciers, in the north and in the south, with their voluminous lowering of the ocean waters, were the keys that caused Pangaea's division.

What were the post-Flood climatic conditions that created the glaciers? These are the probable factors: The original creation appears to have had a transparent water vapor "greenhouse" atmosphere.[4] The rainfall of the Flood removed most of that water vapor. The loss of that greenhouse created a new atmosphere. That is, instead of a mild, temperate pre-Flood world throughout, the climate became hot in the low latitudes and very cold in the high latitudes. The world was no longer pleasant throughout as it was before the Flood. For example, warm weather fossils are found in Antarctica and Greenland, indicating a temperate pre-Flood climate in the polar regions.[5] Hot and cold harshness in many areas became new environments, an extension of the Curse.

The ocean had residual heat released from the rain and the hot seismic action of the Flood.[6] With new equatorial heat, internal heat from within the water, and the sun's heat from above, extensive evaporation of ocean water began. (Evaporation rates were unusually high over the much less salty ocean.)[7] The remains of volcanic dust in the atmosphere from the Flood's crustal disturbances augmented the condensation of the water vapor into snow. (Water condensation needs microscopic particles.[8]) Furthermore, geologic evidence reveals that extensive volcanic activity continued after the Flood, its dust producing significant climatic cooling.[9]

Pangaea's ocean almost certainly had not yet developed what are called the "global conveyer" phenomena. (One example of these phenomena is the Gulf Stream, "the North Atlantic conveyer," the stream that warms Northern Europe today.) Without conveyer polar warming, glaciers would more readily develop.[10] Finally, the normal hot to cold, equatorial to polar air patterns moved the water vapor toward the poles where it condensed and fell as snow. Furthermore, continental glaciers, once begun, tend to be self-perpetuating. See chapter 13, footnote 16. These probable factors produced the immense glaciers.[11]

Regardless of the causes, the Glacial Epoch developed over a considerable period. (We see on Greenland and Antarctica the remains of those extensive glaciers. See figure 33.) As we have stated, glacial rock debris indicates that those massive ice caps covered much of Pangaea. That transportation of "permanent" water-mass to North and South Pangaea generated global instabilities. These forces and the energies they stored finally caused extensive crustal changes including Pangaea's division.

In the next chapter, we will examine the unusual global developments that came after the Flood.

Chapter 3 Footnotes

1 - An important fact: Almost all of a continent's mass is below sea level. That means that almost all continental dry lands are relatively near sea level. Therefore, flooding Pangaea was very doable even without the rain.

2 - Charlesworth, Vol 1, 211.

3 - A dumbbell is a short bar with weights at each end that is held by one hand and used for exercise.

4 - 5th ICC , 29. Questions exist concerning the pre-Flood surface temperatures that the greenhouse atmosphere produced. See also 2nd ICC, 231. To keep the temperatures from getting too hot, God may have used a moderate, partial cloud cover. Furthermore, clouds are usually esthetically pleasing to the eye, and comforting, a blessing to Adam and Eve.

That pre-Flood atmosphere was probably carefully balanced, with the strong potential for the eventual run-away collapse and rainfall of the Flood.

5 - Nature, March 11, 2004, 114-115

6 - Vardiman, 1996, 94. Also, Vardiman, 2001

7 - Continental runoff makes the oceans continually saltier.

8 - Morris et al, 308

9 - Nature, March 24, 2005, 456

10 - "A Constant Conveyor": Science, May 7, 2004, 456

11 - Uniformitarian theories that seek to explain how the Glacial Epoch developed are very inadequate. They lack the dynamics to produce the snowfalls needed to remain throughout the summer melting seasons, the basic requirement for continental - not mountain - glacier formation. That is, their theories lack the elements for getting the continental glaciers started; they lack the catastrophic foundation needed for the Glacial Epoch.

The following possible run-away phenomena are instructive, one subtracting and one adding: Many scientists are concerned that global warming may "tip the point" at which ice melting reaches run-away levels. That is, new heat will be absorbed into the Artic waters because of the loss of radiant-heat-reflection caused by the disappearing white Artic ice due to melting. This would result in a new heat-absorption-ice-melting cycle increasingly feeding itself. This sequence would produce run-away warming.

Such a run-away melting possibility is instructive concerning the opposite phenomena: the probability that the Glacial Epoch resulted from run-away cooling together with prodigious snowfalls. See, "Could climate change run away with itself?" Nature, June 15, 2006, 802.

4 - The Magnitude of Changes

One of the 20th century's leading authorities concerning the Glacial Epoch, J.K. Charlesworth, made this assertion regarding the crustal movements that occurred during the Glacial Epoch, the Pleistocene: "The Pleistocene indeed witnessed earth-movements on a considerable, even catastrophic scale. There is evidence that it created mountains and ocean deeps of a size previously unequalled….The Pleistocene indeed represents one of the crescendo in the earth's tectonic [mountain building] history."[1] Concerning the great tectonic movements of the Pleistocene, Richard Flint, another leading geologist of the 20th century, said, "…the world wide distribution of these [mountain] movements is striking."[2] What evidence prompted Charlesworth and Flint to make these strong statements? The evidence is in the folding, the faulting, the elevations, and the upheavals of the sedimentary rocks *and* the deformed glacial remains on them. Intense crustal forces distorted the sediments and those glacial remains *after* those sediments and remains were horizontally deposited. In this section, we will explain the importance of that evidence.

First, some background. Concerning the Flood the Word says, "…the world that then existed was deluged with water and perished." (2 Peter 3:6) From the data given in Genesis 6-8, the Flood was universal. All of Pangaea was devastated and very deeply eroded. The Flood created many different kinds of sediments. From those sediments the permanent stratigraphic rock record began. Pressure, heat, and cementing agents hardened those sediments into various kinds of rocks: sandstone, limestone, mudstone, shale, coal, etc. It undoubtedly took many years for all the geologic processes, so violently initiated during the Flood year, to settle down for the gradual hardening of the sediments. Beside the eroding processes, crustal changes occurred during the Flood. However, the overall sedimentary results were of the form shown in figure 2. (See also figure 4A) That is, gravity determined the initial orientation of the sediments, and therefore the sediments were laid parallel to the earth's surface. Therefore, level-lying, horizontal, sedimentary rocks, like the pages of a book on a table, characterized the earth's original stratigraphic record. This fact is very important. Knowing the initial, general orientation of strata helps to unravel the sequence of the changes in the continental crust, and the approximate time when Pangaea's division and separation occurred.

While the post Flood sedimentary, level formations were being solidified, equatorial waters were being evaporated and snow was falling in the polar regions. The snowfall must have been exceedingly great. All the conditions were excellent for this "mass transportation." Furthermore, as the snowfall continued, the evidence reveals that the oceans were lowered by evaporation 650 feet and probably more.[3]

It is not difficult to determine the extent of the removal of ocean water by evaporation: Lowering the seas produced new dry lands and shorelines. Forms of life live on dry land and in shallow seas, leaving their remains. Thus, over 400 feet below the present sea level we find, for example, the following remains: submerged coral reefs, sediments, sills, peat layers, swamps, pollen, tree stumps, roots, and submerged shorelines.[4]

17

Appalachian Plateau, near Pittsburgh

Grand Canyon, Colorado Plateau

Original post-Flood horizontal strata
Figure 2

With a drop in sea level of at least 650 feet (400 + 250 = 650; see footnote 3), that mass movement of water was, geologically, exceedingly effective. Water covers about 71% of the earth's surface. *With the removal of water to a depth of 650 feet from such a large surface area - an enormous volume - and its displacement to the two high latitudes of Pangaea, that unnatural relocation of those masses produced a very unstable earth. Those glaciers, circling at 15 degrees per hour, produced great destabilizing inertial forces.*[5]

Assuming one-third of Pangaea was covered with glaciers and those glaciers were uniform in height, the thickness of the glaciers, in the north and in the south, would have averaged about 5300 feet.[6] Moreover, we know that ice thicknesses were not uniform. Crustal depressions tell us that. The geologic evidence indicates that, in the central parts, the glaciers were in the order of two to three miles thick. (The maximum ice depth on Greenland today is over two miles, and in some regions of Antarctica the ice depth is over three miles.[7]) One measurement of the thickness of the North American ice mass can be made by Mt. Washington, a granitic mountain in New Hampshire. Mt. Washington, whose height is 6288 feet, was covered by the glaciers.[8] The center of the North American ice mass that eroded the top of Mt. Washington must have had a height that was much greater, because the center of the glacier that covered Mt. Washington was at least 800 to 1000 miles to the north.[9]

In addition, the two centers of gravity of the north and south Pangaean ice masses were, almost assuredly, far from the rotation axis of the earth.[10] With a rotating earth, global instability became very great. Moreover, not only did that unstable potential gradually develop but, as Charlesworth and Flint observed, that instability finally produced unusual global crustal movements and mountain building during the Pleistocene, together with volcanic activity and basaltic extrusions onto the surface of the earth. We will analyze the causes for those instabilities. First, we need to examine in detail the extensive deformations that developed during the Ice Age.

Chapter 4 Footnotes
1 - Charlesworth, Vol.2, 603-607.
2 - Flint, 514-515.
3 - Plummer et al, 448. (Estimate of 650+ feet)
   Science, April 15, 2005, 361, 401 (Estimate of 650+ feet)
Though the estimates of the water-mass transfer of the Glacial Epoch vary, these two estimates above of 650' are reasonable. Sea level was highest at the close of the Flood, because the glacial build up began after the Flood. That high sea level is our reference. The following is a common estimate: Consider just the ice stored on Greenland and Antarctica today. (For Antarctica, see figure 33.) Melting Greenland's glaciers would raise sea level by about 23', and melting Antarctica's glaciers would raise sea level by about 230'. Therefore, melting both, the sea level would rise by 253'. If the ice mass at the Glacial Epoch's maximum was at least three times today's ice mass, the sea level drop from our reference would have been about 760 feet [3 x 253 = 759]. Another estimate from melting both glaciers is 260 feet, producing a drop of 780 feet.

(Nature, Mar. 11, 2004, 115). Furthermore, if we included all the world's glaciers, the drop in sea level would have been greater.

Here is another analysis: One study estimates that during the Glacial Epoch, sea level reached 410' lower than at present (Nature, Sept 1, 2005, 126.). Assuming that the present sea level would rise an additional 250' if those two glaciers melted, the sea level would have been 660' feet lower at the Glacial Epoch's maximum. Another estimate: "During the last glacial maximum, global sea level was about… [430 feet] lower than it is today." (Chernicoff et al, 532) This would produce a drop of about 680 feet.

Finally, this summary statement by Henry Morris, who was a leading Christian scientist and authority, is significant. "The total amount of water locked up in these great glaciers during their greatest extent is not known as yet, but it may have been very great….In the past decade [about 1950] a large amount of evidence has been amassed to show that ocean levels were at least 400 feet lower than at present, possibly much more, as shown by such features as the continental shelves, sea-mounts, submerged canyons and terraces, etc." (Morris et al, 294.)

Therefore, the estimate of at least 650' is very reasonable.

4 - Science, May 12, 2000, 1034.

5 - That enormous volume equaled the volume of 360 <u>rectangular</u> "blocks," each block 500 miles long, 50 miles wide and 10,000 feet high. Excluding plateaus, one block probably had more volume than any present mountain range. Furthermore, consider the volume and mass of *360* blocks each filled with water!

6 - The height of the ice is calculated as follows: If the oceans covered 71% of the earth's surface, then Pangaea covered 29%. If the ice mass covered 33% of Pangaea, then glaciers covered 9.66% of the earth's surface. Calculating just the volume of water transported and assuming a 650 foot drop in sea level, then (9.66 times height on Pangaea) = (71 times 650'). Therefore, the average height on Pangaea must have been 4777 feet of liquid water. Because ice is nine-tenths as dense as water, the average glacial height must have been over 5300 feet.

7 - The average depth of the glaciers on Antarctica is 7220 feet. (National Geographic Magazine, Aug. 1977, 188.) For other estimates see, Science, October 13, 2000, 233, "Thicker Ice Sheets," and Science, July 8, 1994, 189, "How High Was Ice Age Ice? A Rebounding Earth May Tell" and 195, "Ice Age Paleotopography."

8 - The altitude at the base of Mt. Washington is less than 500'. Therefore, the ice thickness at Mt. Washington was more than a mile.

9 - The centers for those glaciers were probably north of the Hudson Bay and Labrador regions of Canada. The glacier's movements against Mt. Washington tapered the entire northern side of the mountain. See the article, "Problems" in the appendix concerning Pangaea's original mountains.

10 - The center of gravity (CG) is the point in a body where its weight appears to be concentrated.

5 - Strata Deformation and Mountain Building

Before examining the deformations of the crust that the displaced Ice Age waters produced, we need to examine the depositions the Flood produced. Knowing the purpose of the Flood was destruction and studying Genesis 7:11, we discern that the Flood's seismic movements caused extensive changes in the earth's underlying crust and therefore changes in the sediments settling on the surface. Moreover, apart from the new developing glaciers and their effects, the crust and sedimentary layers on the crust undoubtedly continued to readjust themselves for many years after the Flood. Evidences of the near post-Flood crustal changes appear in some strata formations. A small percentage of the original sediments, though essentially level, were not laid like pages in a book. Figure 3 is a simple, hypothetical, but typical example of depositional sequences that were produced by changes in the elevations of the crust below the sediments.

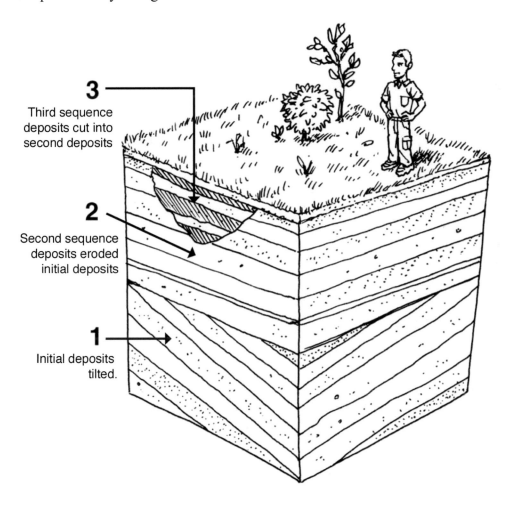

3
Third sequence deposits cut into second deposits

2
Second sequence deposits eroded initial deposits

1
Initial deposits tilted.

Original depositions altered by near post-Flood crustal movements
Figure 3

To produce the sequences of the depositions shown in figure 3, elevations in the crust below the deposits had to be changing to alter the sediments' orientations and to make the waters go, first, one way and then another. Furthermore, the erosion sequences shown in figure 3 (for example, the cutting of previously laid sediments) had to happen before those sediments became hard. In summary, many crustal changes below the sediments occurred during the Flood and some changes during the near post-Flood period to produce such complex layering. Crustal changes produced a variety of depositional patterns. The stratigraphic record has many variations.

However, the predominant and extensive stratigraphic record throughout the world was, initially, that which was described in Chapter 4. Figure 4A expresses that important principle: level-lying sedimentary rock was the normal formation, especially in the centers of the continents. For example, horizontal strata predominate throughout Middle America, from the Appalachian Plateau to western regions like the Colorado Plateau and the Northern Rockies. See figure 2. On the Colorado Plateau, this horizontal phenomenon expresses itself beautifully in the Grand Canyon and in the Plateau's other marvelous horizontal strata formations. We must emphasize this principle: level-lying strata characterized the world's original near post-Flood sediments.

With that principle firmly in mind, we see in today's deformations that drastic changes convulsed the crust of the earth *since* those initial sediments were laid, that is, since the Flood and near post-Flood period. One geology textbook describes these deformations well: "The surface expression of plate movement is dramatically shown in the intense deformation of the crust in the great mountain belts of the world, where thick sequences of sedimentary rock that *accumulated as horizontal layers*…are now folded and faulted to form the highest mountains on Earth." [1]

The second principle to have firmly in mind is that great forces produced these drastic changes. Though there are exceptions, significant deformations are usually found in the outer regions of the continents, that is, on the edges of the earth's plates, and in the few regions where the edges of a plate penetrate a continent.[2] What are the characteristics of these deformations?

Figures 4B through 6 describe the three basic types of mountains of deformed strata. (Except for the remnants of pre-Flood mountains, volcanic mountains are the only other mountain types.) Figure 4B, "Fault-Block Mountains," is typical of many mountain ranges, such as the Rockies, the Swiss Alps, and the Himalayas. See the examples in figure 5. Note that these "blocks" have been heavily weathered and eroded. To create this type of deformation required that the sediments be sufficiently hardened to withstand crustal forces that faulted and then elevated them. However, some residual plasticity can be seen in these elevated sediments. Figure 5 is an example of bent strata in Fault-Block Mountains. These elevations, with some residual plasticity, reveal that in terms of time, this type of mountain building was after the Flood and yet not too far removed in time from the Flood period.

Figure 4C, "Folded Mountains," is typical of other mountain ranges, such as the Appalachian Mountains. (Contrary to the usual time-scale, the Appalachians are "young." [3]) See the example in figure 6.[4] Like Fault-Block deformations, this type of deformation shows that the sediments were only partially hardened when crustal forces bent them.

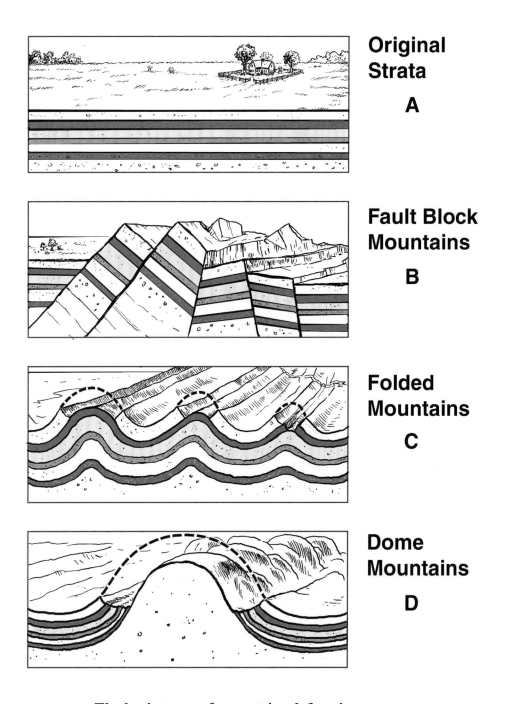

Original Strata

A

Fault Block Mountains

B

Folded Mountains

C

Dome Mountains

D

The basic types of mountains deforming strata
Figure 4

If the sediments had been fully hardened, the great compressive stresses wanting them to bend would have fractured and crushed the sedimentary rock or changed the sedimentary rock to metamorphic rock.[5,6] The bending of strata shown in figures 4C, 5 and 6, are very common throughout the stratigraphic world.

23

The structure of figure 4D, "dome mountains", was produced when magma was forced up through the strata. These protruding formations are typical of much of the Cascade and Sierra Nevada Mountains. See the example in figure 6.

Fault-Block Mountains:
Upper : **Northern Rockies.**
Lower : **Canadian Rockies, with residual plasticity**
Figure 5

Upper : **Folded Mountain, Appalachian syncline, Maryland**
Lower : **Dome Mountain, Sierra Nevada Mountains**
Figure 6

25

Over the long years of weathering, erosion has removed many layers of strata from all the strata-deforming mountains resulting in their truncated forms.

The fault structures shown in figure 4B are very common. Faults of various kinds exist throughout the stratigraphic world. These three types of deformations, with faults, are combined in countless ways, from mild deformations to extreme deformations.

We need to keep in mind this fundamental principle: after a considerable interval following the Flood, after the horizontal formations were laid, tremendous forces bent, faulted, distorted, and elevated the hardening sediments. One geology textbook expresses this fact clearly: "*All* the great mountain chains of the earth include folded sedimentary rocks as a conspicuous part of their structure."[7] This fact reveals the post-Flood development of mountains. The level-lying sediments of the Flood, as they were being hardened, were then pressed, pushed up and down, folded and faulted by great crustal forces. Peleg's day began a cataclysmic time! We will examine the timing, the forces, the energies, and the power, needed to produce those changes.

Having described these geologic pictures, we can make this firm assertion: Almost all mountains of the world were formed after the Flood and during the period of the Glacial Epoch. For examples, see Chart 1. The Ice Age was a time of mountain building; it was, geologically, incredibly active.[8]

How do we know that this is true? Because, (1) the level-lying Flood sediments had to have time to harden sufficiently, and (2) mountain building forces changed the orientation of the horizontal sedimentary layers, especially with glacial deposits on them, altering them into new angles and folds, all *after* the sediments were laid and the glacial remains deposited. Therefore, almost all mountains had to be formed during the Ice Age.

Speaking of mountain building during the Glacial Epoch, Richard Flint said: "In North America…movements involving elevations of thousands of feet are recorded in Alaska and in the Coast Ranges of Southern California." Flint then lists Glacial Epoch mountain building in Scandinavia, the Alps, in Turkistan, the Caucuses, in Central Asia, the Himalayas, the Andes, and in Eastern Africa.[9]

Concerning the geologic activity of the Glacial Epoch, J.K. Charlesworth wrote: "Faulting, uplift and crustal warping have been proved for almost all quarters of the globe. Faults…have been observed in many countries traversing glaciated rock-surfaces, drifts, tills, moraines, outwash faces, loess, varved clays, etc." (See chapter 13 concerning these glacial phenomena.) He asserts that this great geologic activity, during the Pleistocene, affected 70% of the total earth surface.[10]

Concerning the Pleistocene period of mountain building, O.D.von Engeln and K.E. Castor said: "…Pleistocene diastrophism [mountain building] is perhaps the greatest and most widespread that the earth has known since Pre-Cambrian times [a secular period approximately 600 million years before the Pleistocene]." "[During the Pleistocene] great volcanic activity was an accompaniment of this up heaving in many localities…."[11]

These geologists affirm that our mountains were built during the Glacial Epoch. These phenomena reveal the results of the great forces and energies that also divided Pangaea. We will elaborate on these conditions.

Chart 1

These are a few of the many mountain ranges that were formed after the Flood: [12]

North America
        Rockies   Appalachians
        Sierra Nevadas   Cascades
        Bighorns   The Coast Ranges

South American
        Ecuadorian, Bolivian, and Chilean Andes

Europe
        Alps   Urals
        Caucasus Mtns   Carpathian Mtns
        Apennines   Pyrenees
        Sudeten Mtns   Jura Mtns

Asia
        Himalayas   Kunlun Mtns
        Taiwan Mtns   Japanese Mtns
        Tien Shan Mtns   Shanxi Mtns

Africa
        Ruwenzori Mtns

SW Pacific
        New Zealand Mtns   New Guinea Mtns

In their book, The Origin of Mountains, Cliff Ollier and Colin Pain make these significant statements. "It is remarkable that mountains in many parts of the globe, all characterized by rapid uplift after a period of rapid planation [erosion that created horizontal sedimentary rocks] should occur in so many different tectonic styles [types of mountains]....Why should a near-global pulse of mountain building take so many different forms?....And why should a period of tectonic quiet [period of erosion and deposition] be followed so rapidly by a period of great uplift?....We do not yet know what causes this short, sharp period of uplift, but at least the abandonment of naïve mountain hypotheses might lead to further realistic explanations."[13]

These decisive statements and the concluding admission by Ollier and Pain are timely and germane. They provide a good conclusion to this portion of our thesis. Their statements of "rapid uplift," "near-global pulse of mountain building," "a period of great uplift," and "this short, sharp period of uplift" refer to the secular Pleistocene period of mountain building, i.e. what we are asserting to be the post-Flood mountain building period of the Glacial Epoch. These statements by Ollier and Pain support our thesis. Furthermore, their admission of ignorance as to the causes of this period of mountain building, and their candid assertion of the inadequacy of the theory of long-age plate tectonics to explain these recent mountain building phenomena is very instructive.[14] The secular theory of plate tectonics requires many millions of years to produce continental movements and deformations. Yet, geologists recognize this momentous Pleistocene period of mountain building. Secular geology, with its plate tectonics theories, has no explanation for the extensive mountain building during the "short period" Pleistocene and furthermore, no explanation for the *absence* of mountain building for millions and millions of years before then.

In additions to these evidences concerning mountain building, we will present other evidences in support of the geologic instability that developed after the Flood. Geologic fingerprints support the thesis that the intense deformations of mountain building were part of the Pleistocene's division of Pangaea. The clearest evidence that Pangaea divided during the Glacial Epoch, however, will be given in Chapter 13, particularly from the evidence associated with "the southern ice mass."

The purpose of this long study of post-Flood mountain building is to show that the forces that built the mountains were the very forces that divided Pangaea. Having described these significant earth movements, we now need to explain the sources of the forces and energies that caused global mountain building and Pangaea's division.

Chapter 5 Footnotes

1 - Hamblin et al, 460.

2 - Two examples of the few regions where plates penetrate continents: the Pacific Plate sliding by the North American Plate, producing the San Andreas Fault that runs north-south through western California; the Arabian Plate separating from a splitting African Plate, producing the Great Rift Valley that runs north-south through most of eastern Africa and into the Middle East. For an elaboration see chapter 8, footnote 5.

3 - "The topography of the Appalachians is geologically quite young." Plummer, 515.

4 - A syncline fold is U-shaped. An anticline fold is arch-shaped.

5 - Speaking of hardened rock, the following assertion is significant: "It cannot be over-stressed that it is not possible to fold rocks by a lateral push….If a sufficiently large force were somehow applied to such a slab, it would not move, but would simply be crushed at the point where the stress was applied." "…the strength of rocks is insufficient to permit folds to be created by lateral compression." (Ollier et al, 275.) These statements support the fact that the post Flood sediments were not yet fully hardened when forced to bend. These statements reveal the inadequacies of secular theory to explain folding.

6 - As we have emphasized, the absence of crushing and metamorphism in the many folded sedimentary rocks indicates that they were folded while they were still flexible. Therefore, the rocks could not have been millions of years old. This evidence contradicts the evolutionary theory that it took millions of years to form those sedimentary layers. We see this plasticity in all strata-deforming mountain ranges; these sediments still had pliability before solidification. (Science, July 9, 2004, 233, 161, 237.) Note: In the midst of sedimentary rock supposedly two to three hundred million years old, soft clay layers still exist, which indicate that that hardened rock is not old.

Metamorphic rock is rock produced by molding previous rock by pressure and heat during which that rock's previous structure is lost. (Some portions of the Appalachians did become metamorphic.) The following processes give the origin of some metamorphic rocks: due to heat and pressure, granite and basalt both produce schist and gneiss, shale produces slate, limestone produces marble, and sandstone produces quartzite.

7 - Longwell et al, 460. Therefore, *all ranges were formed post-Flood*!

8 - Concerning "Mount Ararat" of the post Flood period (Gen 8:4) and other pre Flood mountains, see the Problems article in the appendix.

9 - Flint, 514-515.

10 - Charlesworth, Vol 2, 603-607.

11 - Von Engeln et al, 439.

12 - Chart 1 incorporates data from the Institute for Creation Research article, "When Did The Mountains Rise" by Morris, J.D., No. 195, March 2005, El Cajon, CA.

13 - Ollier et al, 273, 302-303.

14 - The supposed millions-of-years processes of plate tectonics did not produce the short period of mountain building that occurred during the Glacial Epoch. Secular geology should recognize that the unique period of mountain building during the Pleistocene is highly inconsistent with their doctrine of uniformitarianism, *the present is the key to the past*. If their theories were true, mountains should have always been building somewhere.

The Crucial Issue

Accepting only natural causes to explain the stratigraphic evidence, many scientists fail to perceive important geologic characteristics. They dismiss the Genesis Flood maintaining that

1 – Sediments took a very long time to form and to harden, and

2 – Most sediments were not flood type, but a mix of marine, wind blown, lake and evaporative deposits.

With these convictions, they reject the previous catastrophic explanation for strata.

However, many scientific books and articles explain how the Genesis Flood produced these sediments.* Moreover, only catastrophic processes explain many, if not most sediments. The history of the global Flood is crucial for geology. Concerning our thesis, the post-Flood environment ultimately produced the instabilities that caused mountain building and Pangaea's division.

* Among these helpful books are the following:
- Scientific Creationism (Chapter 5), Morris, H.M., editor, Master Books, © 1985
- Grand Canyon, Monument to Catastrophe, Austin, S.A., editor, Institute for Creation Research, © 1994
- Origin By Design, Coffin, H.G., Brown, R.H., Gibson, L.J., Review and Herald Publishing.

6 - Conservation of Angular Momentum

The thesis of this book is that the "permanent" relocation of enormous water masses in the two high latitudes created instabilities that resulted in the division of Pangaea. We will analyze that division later. First, we need to determine how that relocation of masses created instabilities.

The earth is a rotating sphere subject to the laws of rotation. One law it must obey is the Law of the Conservation of Angular Momentum. To explain this law, lay a bicycle on its side and spin its front wheel. A good wheel will rotate for a long time. (Without friction and air-drag, the wheel would rotate forever.) That rotating wheel demonstrates the principle of the conservation of angular momentum. The word "conservation" simply means "the keeping of." With no frictional losses, momentum cannot be lost.

The rotating wheel's mass, how that mass is distributed, and its angular velocity, determine the wheel's angular momentum. Assume a rotating wheel with no friction. In order to keep its angular momentum constant, any change in the distribution of its mass requires that the rate of rotation change also. Therefore, while the wheel is rotating, if somehow the radius of the wheel were reduced, the wheel would have to rotate faster to maintain its angular momentum. In fact, if its radius were reduced by half, the wheel would have to rotate four times as fast to keep (conserve) its momentum. We see this phenomenon with a rotating figure skater: he draws in his arms and legs reducing the radius of his mass and, conserving his angular momentum, he spins like a top.

(To demonstrate this conservation law, take a friend to a local park and together use its merry-go-round. Have your friend sit on its platform while you make the merry-go-round rotate. After picking up speed, jump on and then pull yourself toward its center. [You will have to pull hard, and harder as you approach the center.] The merry-go-round will pick up speed and rotate so fast that your "friend" will probably end up in the grass. See figure 7. Please tell your friend what you plan to do! Tell him that he is "Pangaea" and you are "Ice." The deficiency of this experiment for our purposes is that, historically, when Pangaea divided, its glaciers, which rode on Pangaea's back, went flying too.)

The most effective factor of the Conservation Law is not the mass, nor the rate. The most effective factor is the distribution of the mass. This fact also applies to the earth. The most effective part of the earth determining its angular momentum is its crust, because the crust is the part furthest from the axis of rotation.[1]

Moving water by evaporation and air currents from the equatorial regions toward the poles, that is, toward the earth's axis of rotation, shortened the radii from the axis to those masses of water. Thus, fixing water in glaciers nearer the earth's axis produced the results of making - or trying to make - the earth rotate faster. Because of their surface locations, those glacial "pushes" were very effective. What is important is that this rotational phenomenon produced a significant secondary result: in trying to push the earth to rotate faster, the glaciers produced crustal stresses.

When the north and south glaciers were forming, where were those forces being applied that told the earth to rotate faster? The glaciers applied rotational forces to the crust. Consequently, the crust said to the "big-earth" below the crust, "Go faster!"

Large Radius / Low Rate

Small Radius / High Rate

**Merry-Go-Round experiment: conservation of angular momentum
Figure 7**

However, everything under the crust, being stubborn, said "No way!" The reason for big-earth's resistance to those two north and south crustal forces was that the core and the mantle together, the "big-earth," constitute essentially the entire mass of the earth (99%), and therefore they, not the crust, primarily determined the earth's rotational inertia (its angular momentum), and therefore they controlled the earth's rate of rotation.

31

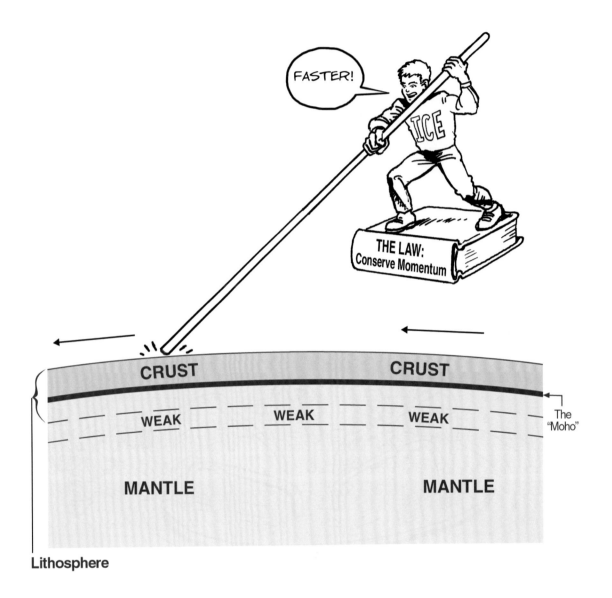

Momentum forces applied to crust
Figure 8

Therefore, a conflict developed between the crust and the mantle: the crust wanted (required!) the earth to go faster, but the mantle did not.

As the glaciers were building above the crust, rotational forces were increasing, stress and energy in the crust, plasticity and heat in the "weak" mantle layer, and the potential for crustal instability were increasing – because of that conflict. The illustration of figure 8 describes this conflict.

Concerning figure 8, understand the following: As the north and south glaciers were building, each of which were applying forces seeking to increase the earth's rotation rate, they were also removing water from the equatorial regions. This removal of low latitude water had the same effect on the earth's rotation rate: removing low-latitude mass also made - or tried to make - the earth rotate faster. Concerning the illustration of figure 8, it is easier to show the addition of mass, i.e. ice, at the high latitudes than the subtraction of water from the low latitudes. But the subtraction dynamics of the Conservation Law were also effective in producing the crust-mantle conflict.

In describing this conflict between the crust and the mantle, we have kept the details simple. The factors in this conflict were more complex.[2] However, we have described the essential factors.[3]

Summarizing: with this glacial water-mass movement, the earth became unstable in maintaining its angular momentum.

Chapter 6 Footnotes

1 - Angular momentum is determined by the rotation rate, the effective mass, and the square of the radius to that mass. Because the radius is squared, angular momentum is especially sensitive to the changes in the radius to that mass.

2 - Because of the different radii from the earth's curved surface to the earth's axis, the conservation of angular momentum forces due to the glaciers were not uniform. That is, because of the radii differences, the glaciers would exert the greatest momentum forces on the crusts at the higher latitudes (smaller radii) and less force at the lower latitudes. Therefore, a coriolis type force field (see below) would produce a twisting of Pangaea's crust. Secondly, the weight of the ice on the high latitudes, and the loss of weight (water) at the low latitudes would compress the crust at the high latitudes and cause the earth to bulge at the low latitudes. This secondary redistribution of mass would partially negate some of the conservation forces produced by the mass-movement of water. However, the new pressure differences would tend to split Pangaea, a subject discussed below.

Coriolis Effect: The earth's surface velocity varies with latitude. Its velocity is approximately 1040 miles per hour at the equator and decreases to zero miles per hour at the poles. The Coriolis Effect is the effect of these velocity differences on masses as they move to or away from the equator. In the case above, the coriolis type characteristics would be due to the variations in radii which, in turn, depend on the latitudes.

3 - The conservation of angular momentum changes can be detected today. See "Oceanic Effects on Earth's Rotation" in Science, Sept. 11, 1998, 1623, 1656. Also see Chapter 14, footnote 3, concerning glacial melting changing earth's rotation rate.

7 - Other Instabilities

Inertial forces were the primary cause for Pangaea's division. One factor that contributed to crustal instability derived from the fact that the earth's mass must obey Newton's First Law of Motion. The First Law states that a mass in motion stays in motion in a straight line unless forced to turn. Thus, our rotating earth wants to fly apart, that is, every bit of its moving mass wants to go in a straight line. However, earth's gravity forces all of its masses to change direction continually. Because of gravity (a centripetal force), the earth's masses hang together.

The surface velocity at the equator is the highest, approximately 1040 mph, while the surface velocity at the poles is zero. Therefore, equatorial masses have the strongest desire to go in a straight line, that is, to fly off. However, with the force of gravity pulling the equatorial masses in toward the earth, a compromise develops between these two Laws, Newton's First Law and the Law of Gravity. As a result, the earth bulges out at the equator while it is shortened at the poles. The elliptical, oblate, shape of the rotating earth is normal. The earth produces its oblate shape by moving mass toward the equator. See figure 9 (using magnified dimensions). It is convenient to think that "centrifugal" forces produce this bulging phenomenon.[1]

Concerning crustal forces, the north and south Pangaean glaciers reversed the normal polar flattening and equatorial bulging of the earth. Moving mass from the low latitudes and "permanently" locating the two ice masses at the high latitudes was exactly opposite to what the rotating earth naturally did. The earth's normal, oblate shape was the earth's stable state, while reshaping the earth by the new glaciers created an unstable state. Therefore, as the glaciers grew, stresses developed in the crust to move mass back toward the equator. The glaciers themselves could not move. However, the two glaciers stressed the land upon which they rode to move toward the equator. See figure 9B. These stresses generated a conflict between the crust of the ice-bearing Pangaea and the mantle below. This conflict grew as the glaciers were growing. Therefore, the stress and energy in the crust, the plasticity and heat in the mantle's "weak" layer, and the potential for crustal instability, such as fracturing, grew.

Now the centers of gravity (CG's) of the north and south glaciers were almost assuredly not on the earth's axis of rotation. Figure 9C describes this more realistic condition. Because the CG's were off-axis, centripetal forces, i.e. asymmetric gravitational forces, developed from the glaciers. Moreover, the earth had to "hang on" constantly to those great revolving masses which wanted to go straight. That pulling was hard work. That pulling, in the north and in the south, inclined the earth to wobble. However, wobbling is not something the big-earth below liked to do. See figure 10, and footnote 2 for an elaboration.[2] Put all these forces together and the big-earth said to the crust, "What are you doing?!" Therefore, the total earth did something about that "problem." It gradually repositioned the masses above the weak layer; it divided Pangaea.

Another phenomenon that contributed to the division of Pangaea is the fact that planet earth is a gyro. As a gyro, planet earth seeks to maintain gyroscopic stability. Stability means that the earth keeps its axis of rotation pointing in a precise direction – toward the North Star. However, with the build up of the two large glaciers, whose CG's were not on the earth's axis, a conflict developed between the crust, especially the land

34

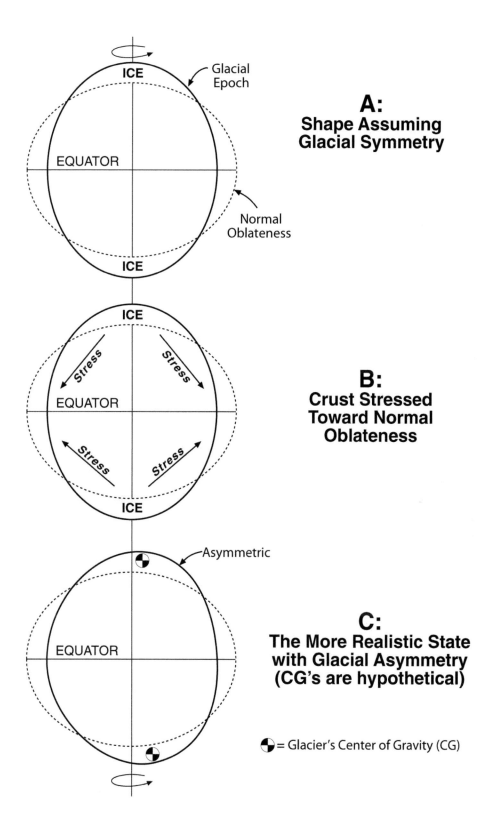

Glaciers changed Earth's shape
Figure 9

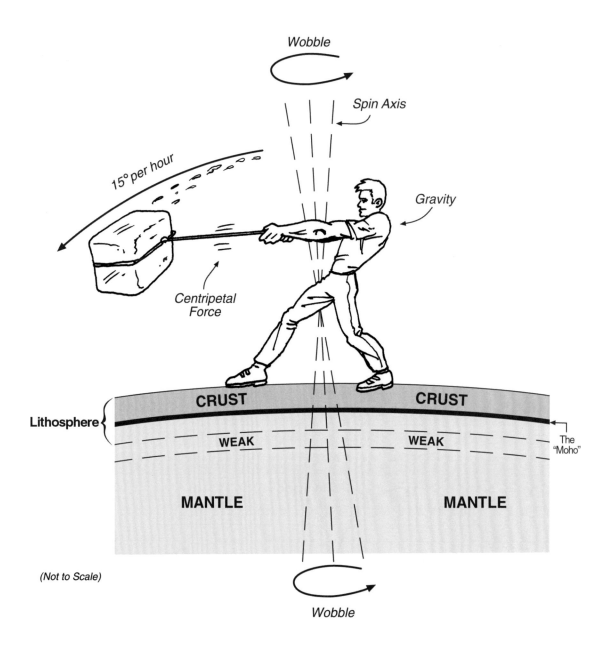

Struggle for stability: 99% of Earth resists wobble
Figure 10

where the glaciers were located, and the big-earth below. That is, the outward tugs of the two glaciers on the north and south ends of the earth were, independently, trying to "precess" the earth, that is, to make the earth tip at 90 degrees to the direction of those tugs.[3] The result was that, with its glacial loads, circling Pangaea tried to pull the earth's

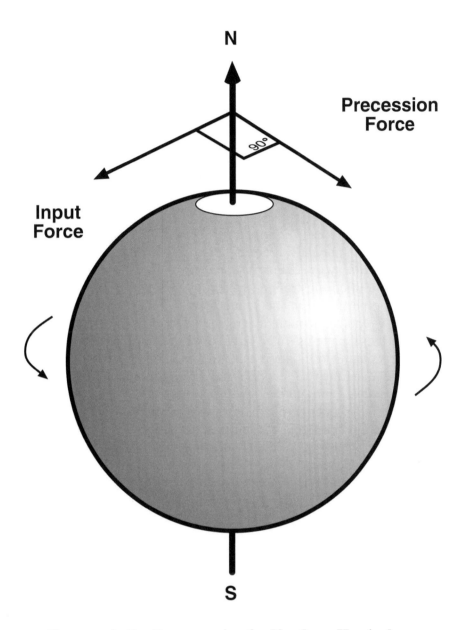

Gyroscopic Earth: precession for Northern Hemisphere
Figure 11

axis away from its normal heavenly direction. See figure 11, which illustrates precession for the Northern Hemisphere. To maintain gyroscopic stability, the big-earth again said to the crust, "No way!" Yet, in hanging on to those glaciers with the centripetal forces of gravity, the big-earth paid a price: those two asymmetric forces added to the earth's inclination to wobble. Of course, 99% of the earth resisted![4] The inevitable result was that all the crust, together with Pangaea and its glaciers, "did their thing": heat increased, lubrication increased, the earth's thin crust deformed, oceanic crust subducted, Pangaea divided, and the new continents, with their glaciers, *slowly* moved across the mantle of the earth. And with all these powerful processes, with surface deformations, mountain ranges developed.

A summary elaboration:

The analyses in this and the previous chapter of the post-Flood destabilizing inertial forces are descriptions in simple, visual and non-mathematical language of phenomena that require rigorous mathematics and physics to express accurately and thoroughly. Furthermore, though the relationships are in fact complex, all the destabilizing forces are manifestations of but *one* dynamic function.

Chapter 7 Footnotes

1 - With respect to rotational motion, centripetal force is a center-directed force. Centrifugal force is an outward-directed force. Centrifugal force is a reaction to centripetal force, the primary force, but the use of centrifugal force is convenient.

2 - Figure 10 is a simplified illustration. In fact, two destabilizing 'pulls' were occurring simultaneously in the north and in the south, forces produced by the circling north and south CG's. These two pulls undoubtedly created a complex force pattern. The dynamics, the feedbacks, of these patterns may have produced resonant conditions (very low frequency, self-perpetuating oscillations), which oscillations would have absorbed and retained very large quantities of energy, and therefore would become highly earth-moving. A mathematical, mechanical analysis may reveal that resonant conditions developed. This oscillatory energy may have been a primary cause for "Peleg's division." See, "The effect of energy feedbacks on continental strength." Nature, July 6, 2006, 67.

3 - When a force is applied to the end of the spin axis of a gyro, an output force is generated that causes the axis of the gyro to move at a right angle to that input force. This right-angle phenomenon is called "gyroscopic precession." The two north and south forces from the gravitational attractions of the off-axis glaciers due to the earth's rotation were both constantly trying to precess the earth. These forces generated complex destabilizing stresses and energies.

4 - Our earth experiences an erratic wobble called the "Chandler Wobble." It has a period of about 433 days, and a polar amplitude of about 10 to 20 feet. It causes are not well understood. Science, August 4, 2000, 710; Science News, Aug 12, 2000. Weather factors can cause minor wobbles. Nature, July 13, 2006, 112.

8 - The Dividing Trigger

We have analyzed several inertial mechanisms that were constantly working to divide and move Pangaea, e.g. the conservation of angular momentum, centrifugal force, and precession. However, a trigger, a breaking point, had to develop for the division to begin. (Keep in mind that the crust of the earth is, in relative thickness and rigidity, like the thin shell of an egg. It is thin and rigid!) That trigger was the great weight of the ice on Pangaea's crust and the up-welling, weakening heat from the weak layer of the mantle.

Geologic evidence exists all over the northern part of the northern hemisphere (and certainly in the southern hemisphere): the weight of that great ice mass depressed the crust of Pangaea, in many places, by several thousand feet. (Today, the ice on Greenland is pressing its crust at least 1,500 feet below sea level. Antarctica's crust in one area is over 8,000 feet below sea level.) With the glaciers now gone, we can measure the depths of those old depressions by observing ancient shorelines now far above water. The crust of the earth throughout Canada, Northern Europe, and Northern Asia is still rebounding.[1] For example, in Stockholm, Sweden, the rate of recovery today is about one centimeter per year, or one meter per century. See figure 12. Extrapolating those recovery rates and measuring the old shorelines, a good estimate can be made as to the depths the ice masses pushed the crust down. The pressures on Pangaea and its depressions were great.

Granite, the core of continents, is brittle. It cannot bend far without fracturing. (Bending a rigid beam down compresses its top but stretches its bottom tending to fracture its bottom.) Moreover, when granite does fracture, the response is much like that of window glass: the fracture explosively spreads. This is probably what happened to Pangaea. With its heavy ice load, fracturing probably began at the bottom at the crust's weakest point. It then propagated rapidly through much if not all of Pangaea. That fracturing was most likely a catastrophic event.[2] Remember that Pangaea was a unit. Therefore, the fracturing patterns that developed in it probably determined the general shapes of the continents that we now have.[3] We can only speculate on those results.[4] Consider this sequence: Once fracturing began, hot magma from below entered the fractures that produced the greatest drops in magma pressure. These contrasting differences in pressure limited the effective separations and thus limited Pangaea's divisions. A major fracture, The Mid Atlantic Ridge, probably began with magmatic intrusions along this north-south opening. See figure 13.

In addition to fracturing, heating the lithosphere by the increasingly hot magmas from the weak layer, the asthenosphere, almost certainly weakened the lithosphere enough to rupture it. We see this weakening phenomenon in action today, e.g. the heat in Eritrea, part of Africa's Great Rift Valley[5]

Once fracturing began, external forces maintained the fracturing and expanded it. Hot magmas from the mantle, under pressure, penetrated the cracks.[6] Glacial pressures forced water down to meet the hot magmas. As the waters met the magmas, explosive pressures resulted, like the pressures of explosive volcanoes. All these factors worked to push the landmasses apart. As the landmasses separated, waters poured into the new

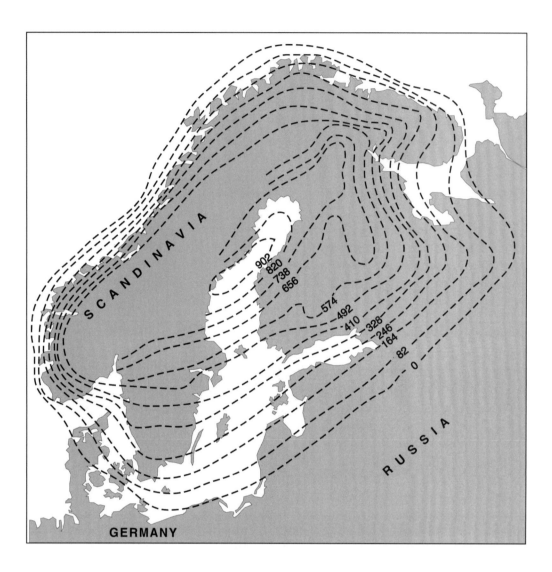

Scandinavian crustal rebound (in feet) from glacial loading
Figure 12

opening ocean basins. Finally, as the continents slowly separated, the glaciers above penetrated into the spreading basins. See chapter 13 concerning the glacial grooves far out in the Artic Ocean, and the glacial debris far from the shores of Antarctica.[7]

With the forces we have described, i.e. momentum, centrifugal force, and precession, and the hydraulic forces from below and above, and the penetration of glaciers – all these factors were in place to divide Pangaea. When the breaking point finally occurred and Pangaea began to separate, the entire crust of the earth must have broken into sections, that is, into plates. (The mechanical freedom of the crust and its isolation from the mantle will be discussed in the next two chapters.) This had to happen because the surface of the earth is space-limited. That is, with new crust being formed between separating continents, the continental crusts and the new and old oceanic crusts had to accommodate each other. A fundamental principle is this: crustal adjustments in one area necessitate an adjustment in a plate(s) somewhere else.

40

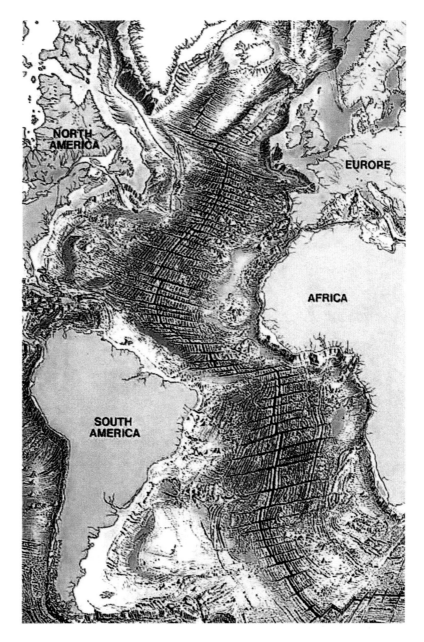

The Mid-Atlantic Ridge
Figure 13

The plates of the earth probably began their existence when Pangaea divided.[8] See figures 14 and 15. Subduction became a new requirement, a new phenomenon. Very powerful earthquakes undoubtedly developed when the earth's plates subducted. (Earthquakes occur when plates make rapid readjustments to each other.) This subject will be developed in Chapter 14.

41

Where new continents were pushing away from each other, and because the granite of continents is lighter, the heavier oceanic plates that were against the continents subducted under the new, lighter continents, forcing up those continental margins. Thus,

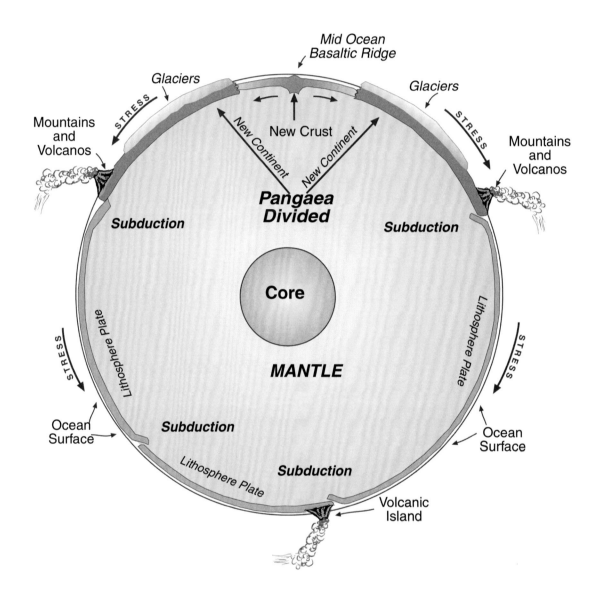

Division and Subduction
Figure 14

mountain ranges formed where those collisions took place. With the heat generated in those collisions, new volcanic eruptions and igneous extrusions were often produced. Most volcanic activity occurs above subduction zones. See figure 14. Examples are the Andes, the Cascades, and the Sierra Nevada mountains, with their many volcanoes, and igneous extrusions, such as the Columbia River Plateau, the Decca Formation, the Karoo-

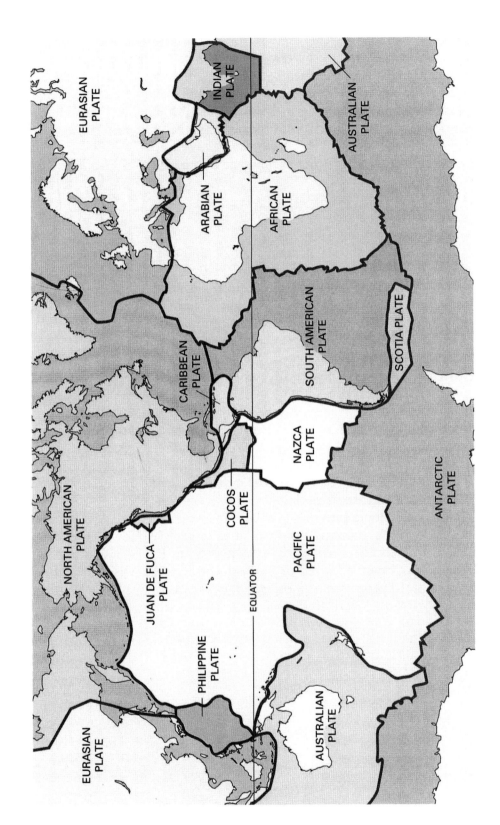

The Earth's Plates
Figure 15
43

Ferrar Flood Basalts, and many others. (See the next section concerning these flood basalts.) In addition, due to Pangaea's separation, the expansion of the earth's crust squeezed many land surfaces within the new continents warping the hardening sediments, for example, the sediments forming the Appalachian Mountains. Furthermore, in many places where the plates collided in oceanic regions, the heat generated produced volcanoes that became islands.[9]

The next chapter analyzes the phenomena of the plates' lubrications.

Chapter 8 Footnotes

1 - For the crustal rebound in North America, see Plummer et al, 430. The rebound of figure 12 is adapted from Longwell, 354.

2 - "Faults greased at high speeds": Nature, Jan 29, 2004, 405.
    "Rupture in the laboratory." Science, Mar 19, 2004, 1788.

3 - A very large earthquake occurred in Scandinavia due to the heavy ice mass of the Glacial Epoch. Science, Nov 1, 1996, 735; Science News, Nov 2, 1996.

4 - "Bursting apart." Nature, Jan 9, 2003, 124. The science of fracturing is part of the sciences of explosives and earthquakes.

5 - "Magma-assisted rifting in Ethiopia." Nature, Jan 13, 2005, 146; "Do Continents Part Passively, or Do They Need a Shove [by subcrustal heat]" Science, Oct 10, 1997, 240. For an elaboration, see chapter 5, footnote 2. See figure 15.

6 - "Magma does the splits." Nature, July 20, 2006, 251, 291.

7 - Water moving into the opening ocean basins may have aided the separations.

8 - A high probability exists that oceanic crust had already been fractured from the previous seismic activity of the Flood. Furthermore, had not those breaks in oceanic crust been in place at the time of Peleg, Pangaea's division could have been more difficult. This is an issue for further research.

9 - Most noticeable geologic activities (earthquakes, volcanoes, etc.) occur at the edges of plates. Inner regions of a plate are usually relatively inactive. However, exceptions exist: Mid America experienced catastrophic earthquakes in 1811-1812. Called "The New Madrid Earthquakes," they occurred in the region where the Missouri and Ohio Rivers join the Mississippi. The causes of these earthquakes may have been from compression stresses due to the North American Plate's movement westward colliding with the Pacific Plate.

9 - Lubrication

Was the crust-mantle interface sufficiently fluid to permit movement of the continents? Actually, was the viscosity below the earth's entire crust low enough to enable global movements? To answer that question we begin with the sediments that existed prior to Peleg. Before Peleg, essentially all sediments were level. Review figures 2 and 4A. If mountain building had been exclusively part of the Flood-year's crustal upheavals, or if mountain building developed immediately after the Flood, the wet and loosely bonded sediments of that deluge period would have been skewed, distorted, or dumped off the elevating granites. The appearance of such (hardened) sediments, would be different than what we see today. Therefore, mountain building came later. On the other hand, at the time of Peleg, the sediments were still not fully hardened, and were not fully "strong" when Pangaea's division and mountain building began. Therefore, being pliable at the time of Peleg, most sediments on the crust would bend without fracturing or melting.

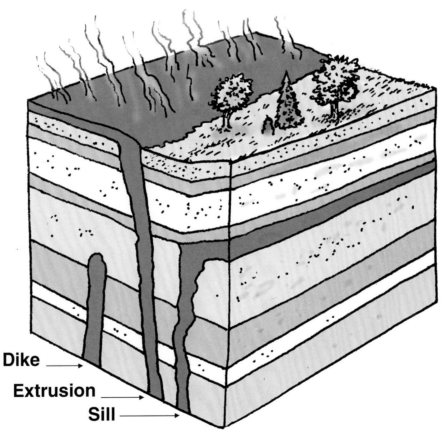

Penetration and extrusion of magmas from hot mantle
Figure 16

At the time of Peleg, major crustal deformations began. When we examine the stratigraphic world, we find "dikes," "sills," and extrusions throughout the crust and sedimentary rocks. Figure 16 describes these intrusions and an extrusion. These magmas came from the hot asthenosphere below. The dikes, sills and extrusions developed after the strata were laid, and while the deformations were made. These formations show that almost all of the intrusions and extrusions penetrating strata came during the period of mountain building. Dikes, sills, and external magmas are prevalent throughout all mountains. See figure 17. Therefore, these intrusions and extrusions came during the

A dike penetrating metamorphic rock, Colorado Rockies
Figure 17

same period when great crustal changes occurred. These phenomena reveal that hot magmas filled the crust-mantle boundary. Indeed, those hot magmas helped lubricate the movement of the new continents.

During this same period of mountain building, in many places the hot mantle poured out extensive magmas onto the surface of the earth. Again, see figure 16. Two immense extrusions were the Columbia River Plateau and the Decca Formation. The Columbia basaltic extrusion in Washington, Oregon, and Idaho, covers about 155,000

46

square miles. It averages 4,000 feet in thickness and is up to 9800 feet thick.[1] The Decca Formation in India is even larger. It covers 500,000 square miles and averages 10,000 feet thick. These extrusions were very hot and fluid when they were rapidly poured out on the land. The Columbia Formation was made by 311 hot layers 15 to 40 feet thick. Those flows traveled nearly 200 miles before they hardened! They came up one right after the other, and therefore are called "flood basalts."

After building the Columbia Plateau, a single eruption to the south, averaging 30 feet thick, covered an estimated 100,000 square miles over parts of California, Nevada, Idaho, and Oregon.[2] This thin and vast eruption must have come rapidly and been extremely hot not to have cooled before covering such a large area. Many very large extrusions like these, catastrophically formed after the Flood, exist throughout the world. These flood basalts reveal that a lot of "grease" was available under the new moving continents.

In considering lubrication and the thermal weakening of the lithosphere from below enabling divisions and movements, the following description of rock fluidity and its magnitude is instructive. "Every once in a while…fissures form in Earth's continental crust and pour forth prodigious quantities of basalt. One way to comprehend the tremendous scale of such events is to note that the average 'flood basalt' would cover the area bounded by New York City, Cleveland, Atlanta, and Charleston [SC] with a slab of basaltic magma over a kilometer thick, burying the Appalachian Mountains to form a broad flat plateau over most of the eastern United States. Why such events occur has been a focus of investigation since the recognition of their huge scale."[3]

Seamounts indicate the abundance of hot magmas right under the crust: Estimates are that the Pacific basin has 30,000 volcanically produced seamounts. Moreover, these seamounts are not grouped together but are widely distributed. Many seamounts exist in all the oceans. These seamounts reveal the extensive hot lubricating magmatic presence just below the crust.[4]

During the Glacial Epoch, extensive volcanic activity existed throughout the earth. Charlesworth states: "Signs of Pleistocene vulcanicity and earth-movements are visible in all parts of the world."[5] These are evidences of magmatic lubrication and crustal forces.

The crust of our earth is shifting every moment; it is restless! Instruments record that the earth is constantly quaking. Like the water tides of the oceans, the gravitational pulls of the sun and the moon are constantly distorting the earth's crust. Our rocky crust has tides too.[6] Heat and fluidity are generated by these distortions – heat is necessary for rock fluidity. On the surface of the earth are many evidences of the extreme heat that exists just below the crust. The crust is still lubricated.

The continents are still moving. New and accurate measuring devices detect continental motion between Africa and South America of about one-half inch per year, i.e. five inches in ten years. Furthermore, in Pacific regions, crustal motions of almost ten inches per year exist.[7] The evidence is that our continents and crusts have moved a considerable distance. They are still moving!

Another factor that was significant in lowering the viscosity of the weak mantle is the existence of water in the mantle. Geologists are confident that water exists in the mantle in very large quantities. One form of water in the mantle is a hydrate, a form in which the water molecule is loosely bound.[8] Water molecules in hydrates can be set free under the right conditions of pressure and temperature. Geologists believe that more water in the hydrate form exists in the mantle than in all of today's oceans.[9] Geologists also believe that the mantle contains great quantities of free water. Volcanoes, with their explosive steams, give us a peek at the mantle's water content. The important principle is that, with an increase in temperature, water is very effective in lowering rock viscosity, that is, in melting the silicates, the dominant mineral of igneous rocks. Water causes already hot rock to melt.[10]

New Global Positioning System sensitivities have detected slow, creeping motions of one plate moving below another. This slow faulting produces minor tremors and are therefore called "slow earthquakes," "slow slip events," and "silent slip events." These measurements reveal how some of earth's plates are adjusting. Water appears to be an important factor in lubricating this smooth slippage.[11]

The evidence is accumulating that the source of hot magmas is in the weak, upper mantle, just below the rigid lithosphere.[12] For additional insight into the lubricating process, see the discussion in the following chapter attending figure 20. All these phenomena indicate that the conditions needed to lubricate the movement of Pangaea's new continents existed. Moreover, our continents are still greased today.

To complete our analysis of crustal movements, we will analyze next the stresses, energies and power required to divide and separate Pangaea.

Chapter 9 Footnotes

1 - Hamblin et al, 662.

2 - Creation Research Society Quarterly, Vol 7, No. 4. Mar.1971, 222.

3 - Science, October 10, 1997, 240.

4 - Science, Nov. 26, 2004. Washington Post, Jan. 24-30, 2005, 35. "Three quarters of the Earth's volcanic activity takes place beneath the oceans." Nature, May 25, 2006, xiii, 494.

5 - Volcanicity: see Charlesworth, Vol 2, 601.

6 - "Crustal Tides," Science, August 27, 2004, 1248.
   "Earth Tides Can Trigger Shallow Thrust Fault Earthquakes." Science, Nov. 12, 2004, 1097, 1164; "Some temblors were probably triggered by [crustal] tides." Science, Dec 4, 2004, 365.

7 - Plummer et al, 481.

8 - The common hydrate is methane hydrate.

9 - Science, Mar 8, 2002, 1885.

10 - Nature, April 7, 2005, 746; May 27, 2004, 356.

11 - Water can help plates slide past each other easily. Also called "silent earthquakes," they do not cause sudden ground motion. Science, May 28, 2004, 1295; Sept 24, 2004, 1917; Water is a lubricating factor. Nature, April 7, 2005, 746; Aug 4, 2005, 689.

12 - "Volcanism a consequence of plate tectonics." Science, May 9, 2003, 921

10 - Energy and Power

The forces we have studied were instrumental in creating the heat needed to produce fluidity. Furthermore, because of the glaciers remaining on the moving continents, these forces continued to push the continents from their initial state of instability into a lower, more stable energy level, that is, into our present state of relative equilibrium.

The source for all instability and energy was the sun. (Energy is the capacity to move an object that resists being moved.) Figures 18 and 19 express this sun-source-

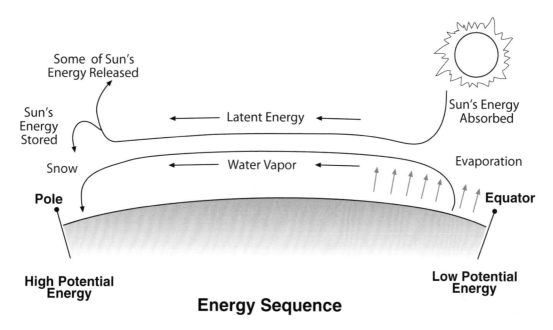

Energy Sequence

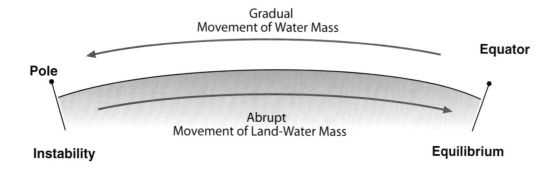

Mass Sequence

The sun, mass and energy
Figure 18

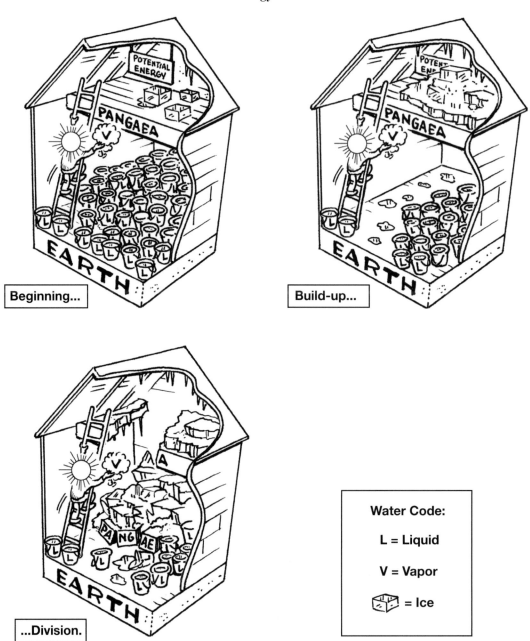

Sun's transport divided Pangaea
Figure 19

movement process. Energy from the sun was absorbed when water evaporated from the low latitudes. Vapor with that latent energy was then moved north and south by weather patterns - also due to the sun - to condense as snow. As snow formed, some of that latent energy was released and went into space. However, some of that energy was retained as snow built the glaciers. Thus, energy from the sun was stored continually as the glaciers grew.

The final mass sequence of figure 18 and the final scene of figure 19 express the results of the breakup of Pangaea: mass was returned "home." The sun was the ultimate source for all that action.

We need to consider a basic phenomenon of physics, that of stress, which is defined below. First a human analogy: we strive to relieve ourselves of stress. The same principle applies in physics: a physical system under stress, if not restrained, responds to remove that stress. Expressed in another way, a high-energy level, if not restrained, goes to a low energy level. Moreover, the higher the energy potential the more the system is inclined to "break down." That describes the overall process that was involved in the breakup of Pangaea. The stored stresses, energies and the growth toward "power" developed as the glaciers were building in the north and in the south. The climax of the Glacial Epoch was not tranquil. Rather, speaking in human terms again, "the situation was getting worse and worse, and something had to be done!"

Figure 18 diagrams that mass-energy sequence from beginning to end. The mass-energy accumulation, shown on the left of figure 18, became critical, and somehow, someway, mass had to be redistributed in order to reduce the stresses and the high energy, unstable levels, back to a state of equilibrium. The "division" sequence of figure 19 illustrates that return.

However, was enough energy and power available to split Pangaea, drive the continents apart, and distort the surfaces of the continents with new mountains? Assuredly, the needed energy and power did develop. Here is a reasonable explanation: First, we need to review some basic principles. Applying a force to a body produces stress.[1] If the force squeezes the body, the force produces compressive stress. If the force stretches the body, it produces tensional stress. And if the force twists the body, it produces shear stress. The change in the dimensions of that body due to stress is called strain. Here is an example: put a weight on a spring to compress the spring. The weight produces the stress. The distance the spring moves down is a measure of the strain. If the stress produces a strain that is too great - over strained - permanent deformation will result. (In our example, the spring would not return to its original shape if over strained.) The significance of these principles is this: by compressing the spring, energy is stored in the spring. This energy is called elastic potential energy, and it can be very great. A mechanic working with a powerful spring under stress must be careful as he releases that spring, because a careless release could be explosive from the energy stored in the spring.

With this background, consider the storage of energy in the earth's crust. Because the crust of the earth is completely continuous, applying forces to Pangaea created stresses throughout the entire crust of the earth. Though rock is not very compressible, from our perspective, it is compressible. Moreover, the earth contains a lot of crust. From the forces acting on Pangaea, the stresses that compressed, stretched, or twisted Pangaea stored a tremendous amount of elastic potential energy not only in Pangaea but also throughout the earth's crust. Because of the sun, that energy was stored continuously – everyday. As the glaciers grew, the energies stored continued to increase. (Earthquakes release this stored energy.) This stored energy became great. Like the spring in our illustration, the energies that were being stored were priming the crust of the earth to move explosively.

Secondly, energy was stored in the form of heat in the weak layer of the mantle. When rocks are under stress, heat is produced when stress produces over-strain, changing internal crystalline structures and producing permanent deformations. Furthermore, when slippage occurs within a rock, friction generates heat. Moreover, because the crust of the earth was continuous, heat, plasticity, and fluidity were produced in the weak layer throughout the entire globe, not just under Pangaea.

Thirdly, gravitational potential energy was produced when glaciers piled up. This form of energy is a potential energy of position. See figures 9, 18 and 19. Another aspect of the energy of position was the "repositioning" of waters from low latitudes to their "permanent" locations at the high latitudes. Those masses of frozen water wanted to go back from where they came. Therefore, the "misplaced" north and south glaciers also stored positional energy.

Lastly, the glaciers' build up of rotational (kinetic) energy was a source of stored energy.[2] See figure 10. Other sources of stored energy probably existed.

All the energies that were produced and stored from the beginning of the Glacial Epoch were instrumental in the final division of Pangaea. Stored energies in the lithosphere finally broke Pangaea apart.

Like the shell of an egg, the very thin lithosphere was essentially isolated. The isolation, produced by the weak layer, the asthenosphere, made the storage of energies in the lithosphere possible. If the weak layer had not existed, the various stresses produced throughout the crust would have been transmitted through the lithosphere and into the solid mantle below and therefore lost. The constant application of forces, and the stresses produced, would not have stored energies. However, because the weak, molten layer did exist, it functioned partially to lock in and preserve the accumulated lateral stresses and energies in the rigid lithosphere above; some of the stresses and energies the glaciers generated were continually retained and stored in the lithosphere.[3] In summary, as the glaciers grew, stresses and stored energies grew, and these finally divided Pangaea.

The ability of energy to divide Pangaea depended on the power available. Concerning power we need a little background: Power is the rate of energy expenditure. Both the amount of energy and the rate at which it is used determine the power. For example, if energy is consumed in a short time, the power level is high, and if that same energy is consumed only over a long period, the power level is low. Now apply this principle to our problem: Given the amount of potential energy available (elastic potential energy, positional energy, rotational energy, etc.), the power to divide Pangaea was determined by the time required to consume that energy and to restore, finally, the crust to equilibrium. Therefore, a critical factor for the division was the time factor.

Consider these time factors: First, the splitting of Pangaea, the rapid fracturing of its granite, were explosive events, violent earthquakes. Consequently, that time factor was small. Second, because sliding friction is usually much lower than static friction, once the splitting of Pangaea was initiated, with the "static friction" overcome, moving the continents was easier, and they proceeded over a "greased" mantle that offered less resistance. (For more insight on the issue of resistance, see the discussion concerning figure 20 below.) Therefore, these two critical time factors were small. The great energy available was released and used up in a moderately short period - as "the earth was divided." The very high probability is that the power needed was enough to divide and separate Pangaea.[4]

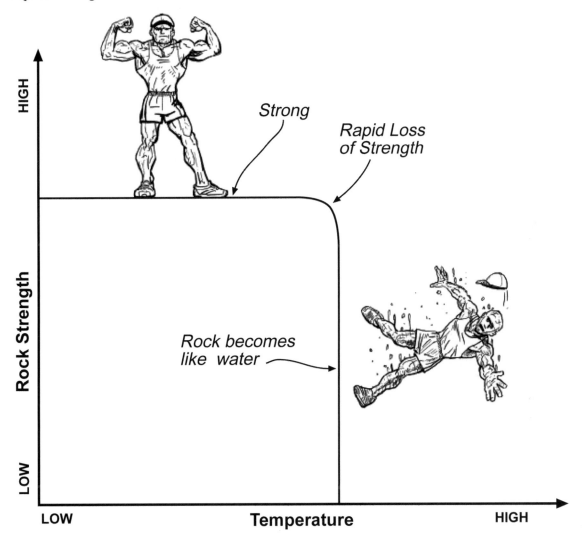

Rock strength determined by temperature
Figure 20

It is important to elaborate on the lubrication, i.e. the reduction of the viscosity of the weak mantle: We could call the lowering of viscosity the loss of rock strength. Figure 20 is very significant. It shows the loss of rock strength as a function of temperature: at low temperatures, silicate-crystalline rock is very strong, but at high temperatures, when the rock begins to melt, the rock rapidly loses its strength. Moreover, when rock does melt, it becomes like water and, essentially, all significant resistance is lost.[5] Loss of rock strength can be a rapid event. Very hot rock can quickly become a lubricant enabling motions of the lithosphere, its plates, and thus continental motion. When resistance is lost, the time factor becomes small and the power level high.

Review the overall time-power factors. The snowfall must have been great, the building of the glaciers expeditious. Sequentially, with forces and stresses building up, the increase in mantle heat was too fast for the heat to dissipate - the time was too short - and therefore mantle heat accumulated. Potential energies accumulated. The forces producing instabilities were "waiting in the wings" to separate the continents. The beginning of the division of Pangaea was a rapid event. Once underway, the continents slowly moved until the supply of energy and the heat had dissipated. Because the time factors were small, and the supply of energy very large, the available power to divide Pangaea was undoubtedly sufficient.

The assurance that the energy and power levels were adequate was rooted in the strong propensity for the northern and southern glaciers to grow continually. Footnote 16 of Chapter 13 explains this propensity. Continual glacial growth produced a continual growth in the destabilizing forces. The growth in forces produced an increase in stresses and a continual increase in the various stored energies. If the growth in stored energies had not ceased, somehow terminated, *the growing potential energies would have reached levels far beyond the energy needed to divide and separate Pangaea.* Therefore, the propensity for the glaciers to grow continually had, finally, to be stopped. The division and separation of Pangaea apparently stopped the glacial growth.

A final observation about the rates at which the continents moved apart: Though the power and energy levels were adequate to initiate movement, it is obvious that the separation rates must have been low. The inertias of such large landmasses were tremendous. Initiating any motion must have taken very large quantities of energy and power. On the other hand, once under way, the inertia of the moving landmasses, with lubrication, would *require* them to travel long distances before all the imparted (e.g. kinetic) energies were consumed.

Chapter 10 Footnotes

1 - Stress is defined as force per area: A force on a large area produces a low level of stress, while that same force applied to a small area produces a high level of stress.

2 - Kinetic energy is the energy of motion.

3 - The following is a simplified, partially accurate explanation concerning the retention and accumulation of stresses and energies. First some background: The phenomena of stress and pressure are equivalent. Both are determined by the force applied to a given area. When an external force was applied to the crust, a stress was generated which was transmitted through it, the lithosphere, to the molten asthenosphere. Because the asthenosphere was enclosed, that is sealed, the stress applied to some area of it became a pressure that was uniformly applied in the asthenosphere. Functioning like a hydraulic chamber, that pressure was transmitted throughout the asthenosphere. Thus, the originally directed external stress lost its directional characteristics at the asthenosphere. That stress was not transmitted through it and directed into the mantle. Moreover, the surface of the asthenosphere, being tensed due to an increase in internal pressure, reflected the external stress back into the lithosphere and therefore was retained.

This simplified explanation needs to be modified. This explanation would have been accurate if the asthenosphere had been a homogenous liquid volume having the viscosity of water, so that pressures applied to the asthenosphere would have been rapidly and uniformly transmitted throughout that layer. However, the liquid characteristics of the molten asthenosphere were heterogeneous and more viscous than water, so that pressure transmissions within that layer were slower and not uniform. Therefore, some external stresses did propagate through that weak layer and into the mantle below. Thus, the asthenosphere only partially reflected external stresses back to the lithosphere. However, the asthenosphere did reflect stresses. Moreover, as external stresses increased, the asthenosphere became increasingly hot, making it increasingly fluid and thus making it increasingly reflective.

See figure 20 and the explanation there for the rapid production of fluidity with increases in heat. For insight concerning the different responses of rock to various stresses, see the discussion of Earth - Seismic Waves in the appendix.

4 - The interval for the secular Glacial Epoch is from about 1,800,000 years B.C. to about 8000 B.C. If that were the time it took to build up and then melt the glaciers, the time factor would have been too long, the mantle heat and the stored energies would have had time to dissipate, and therefore the power level needed to divide Pangaea would have been too low. However, the interval for the actual Glacial Epoch was much, much shorter. The stored energies did not have time to dissipate, and therefore the power levels were high enough to divide Pangaea.

5 - For a technical analysis of viscosities, see Science, Jan 23, 2004, 513, "Viscosity of Fluids in Subduction Zones."

11 - Putting The Pieces Together

This chapter is a concise synopsis that puts all the dividing and deforming elements together: first, the glacial growth, then the dividing forces, and finally the stored energies that pulled Pangaea apart and built the mountains. This summary uses the graph of figure 21. It brings all the factors together sequentially. Using the numbered outline below, this summary begins at the lower left corner of the graph. The time-line is post-Flood.

1 - The sequence leading to the division of Pangaea began with snow falling and building the north and south Pangaean glaciers with water from the ocean.

2 - The glaciers grew to immense sizes. Sea levels dropped significantly.

3 - Destabilizing forces developed and grew. Stresses increased.

4 - Energies began to be stored.

5 - As the glaciers grew and sea levels dropped, the destabilizing forces, stresses and the stored energies grew to a maximum. The explosive point was finally reached and slowly divided Pangaea. Separation probably began at the height of the Glacial Epoch. That explosive point began a long period of crustal deformations, volcanoes, and igneous extrusions throughout the earth.

6 - As the continents began moving apart, some of the glaciers penetrated into the oceans.

7 - The remaining glaciers on the continents began melting. Sea levels began rising.

8 - Because of the remaining glaciers, destabilizing forces were still effective in moving the continents, but gradually those forces decreased.

9 - The stored energies were gradually consumed as the glaciers melted and the continents moved apart. (For example, earthquakes release energy, usually the sudden release of elastic potential energy.)

Our day: far to the right of the timeline of figure 21. These are our conditions:

1 - The north and south Pleistocene glaciers remaining are on Greenland and Antarctica.

2 - Sea levels are still in the order of 250 feet below the initial post-Flood level.

3 - Earthquakes and volcanoes still exist and will probably increase. See chapter 14.

4 - Continental motions are small, but they still exist. See chapter 8.

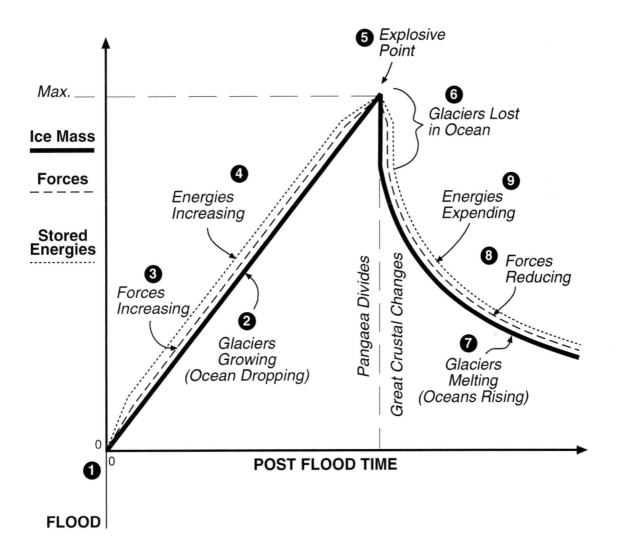

The Dividing Events
Figure 21

12 - Proof of the Division

The geologic evidence for "continental drift" is overwhelming. Pangaea did divide. From the Scriptures, this division began after the Flood, in the time of Peleg. These are some of the convincing physical evidences:

An almost perfect match exists between the eastern boundary of South America and the western boundary of Africa. (Because of the wide variations in the widths of continental shelves, shorelines are visually very misleading. A continent's essential dimensions exist below sea level, at its slope, for example, at the negative 3,000-foot level. See figure 13.) When the continents' slopes are used, Africa and South America fit together beautifully, like a jigsaw puzzle. Without an historical separation, the probability of such continental harmony would have been, essentially, zero.

If Africa and South America were once one land, then along their opposite boundaries, the rock types, the geologic faults, and the veins of ore (tin, copper, gold, iron, manganese, etc.) should match. They do! All of them!

A recent geology textbook states: "Some of the most detailed matches have been made between rocks in Brazil and rocks in the African country of Gabon. These rocks are similar in type, structure, sequence, fossils, ages, and degree of metamorphism. Such detailed matches are convincing evidence that continental drift did, in fact, take place."[1] Other evidence that these southern lands of Pangaea were once joined is the massive formation called the "Karoo-Ferrar Flood Basalts." This extensive magmatic extrusion covered portions of Africa, Antarctica, and Australia before these lands separated. Today these extrusions are thousands of miles apart: all these continents except Antarctica moved northward. Yet these continents carry the same flood basalts.[2]

Very interesting indications of the original unity of Pangaea are found in Scandinavia. Study figure 12. It shows the amount the Scandinavian crust has rebounded since the glacier melted. Notice that along the Norwegian coast the recovery rate changes greatly over a short distance. That fact reveals that the height of the glacier along that shoreline must have been very high and its slope steep. However, the glacier there could not have been high and the slope steep if the ocean had been close, because the glaciers there would have moved into the sea as they developed. That high rebound gradient along the coast indicates that Scandinavia was once part of the Pangaean landmass on its west side. See figures 1 and 32 for that Scandianavian-Pangaean relationship.

The characteristics of the rocks of the Appalachian Mountains, which characteristics continue northeast through Newfoundland, are the same as those of the mountains of the British Isles and of Norway. Pangaea connected all of them.

Two other indications of continental separation: First, the Mid Atlantic Ridge (as a representative oceanic ridge) consists of "divergent-transform faults."[3] Simply, these divergent-transform characteristics indicate the division of Pangaea and the separation of the continents. Furthermore, these fault characteristics indicate that they were rapidly produced and not formed over the millions of years of secular plate tectonics. (Magmas from below entered the opening faults creating new oceanic crust.) See figure 13.

Second, the east-west elevation differences of the Mid Atlantic Ridge (as a representative ridge) indicate that the continents were externally pushed apart rather than internally pulled apart. Secular plate tectonics maintains that the separation of the continents was produced by an up-welling mantle that acted as a conveyor pulling the dividing continents east and west. If that pulling were true, the high probability would be that the oceanic crusts on each side of the ridge would be essentially equal in height. However, they are not. The eastern side is from about 325 feet to 1000 feet higher than the western side. This same condition of higher altitudes on the eastern sides exists throughout the earth's divergent-transform ridges; the eastern sides of the ridges are higher than the western sides. These asymmetries reveal a weakness in the secular theory of continental drift. Rather, these asymmetries are the results of the external asymmetric forces we have identified.[4]

For more geologic evidence, see the article "Historical Conflict and Geologic Evidence" in the appendix. Many other evidences exist such as biological evidences which reveal the original unity and subsequent division of Pangaea. For example, some forms of animal and plant life are essentially the same in Africa and South America, indicating that these lands were once together.

Peleg's Division helps explain both the worldwide distribution of unique animals and the prehistoric evidences of American mankind. (See Folk Lore and History in the appendix.)

Finally, the glacial remains on South America, Africa, India, and Australia reveal that these remains were produced on the southern end of Pangaea before Pangaea divided. That is, these land masses were once joined, and under the one large, southern ice mass. See figure 32. For an extended discussion concerning this evidence of Pangaean unity and its relationship to the southern ice mass, see the following chapter. *Establishing the timing of this relationship establishes the thesis of this book: the division of Pangaea occurred during the Glacial Epoch.*

Chapter 12 Footnotes
1 - Plummer et al, 474.

2 - Nature, September 22, 2005, 454. These flood basalts probably developed as the divisions were commencing.

3 - Divergent-transform fault characteristics: divergent faults (from tensional stress) are joined at right angles by slip faults (from shear stress), i.e. from regions sliding past each other as the lands separated. The Mid Atlantic Ridge clearly manifests these right angle fault characteristics.

4 - Science, July 25, 2003, 438.

13 - Proof of the Glaciers

The central conviction of this book is that tremendous glaciers developed on Pangaea, and that these glaciers and their lowering of the ocean were the factors that split Pangaea and caused it to drift apart. To establish this thesis, the locations, magnitude, and movements of the Pangaean glaciers must be proved. Concerning the evidence of the Glacial Epoch, extensive research has been done and documentation produced, most of which is available in all good libraries. We will not duplicate that extensive documentation. However, here are some of the more impressive phenomena:

Northern Hemisphere glaciers after Pangaea's division
Figure 22

Very large glaciers capped Northern and Southern Pangaea. Moreover, even though Pangaea divided and its landmasses separated, the Glacial Epoch did not suddenly cease. Large continental glaciers continued to function on the northern and southern separating continents. In the Northern Hemisphere, continental glaciers continued to cover much of North America, Northern Europe and Northern Asia. See figure 22. The glaciers of the Southern Hemisphere are described below.

Mountainous regions throughout the world (e.g. The Alps), including mountains in warmer climates (e.g. The Andes), developed extensive mountain glaciers. These phenomena indicate an overall global coolness; after Pangaea's division, the earth's climate partially supported the Ice Age, though the glaciers gradually atrophied.

Consider the North American glacier after Pangaea's separation. Its glaciers covered most of Canada and penetrated south into the United States. The North American glacier came south in phases: advancing, partially melting, advancing, partially melting, each phase covering slightly different areas. Though the exact number and sequencing of the advances are not known, the dominant advances are given appropriate names. In order they were the Nebraskan, Kansan, Illinoian, and finally, Wisconsin. (Pangaea probably began to divide at the height or near the height of the first phase, the Nebraskan.) The southern glaciated areas in the United States are, from east to west: all of New England down to Long Island; all of New York; Northern New Jersey; Northeastern and Northwestern Pennsylvania; all of Michigan; most of Ohio, almost all of Indiana and Illinois; all of Minnesota and Iowa; half of Missouri, the northeastern end of Kansas and the eastern end of Nebraska. From there the edge of the glacier's advance went northwest over much of the Dakotas to Northern Montana and from there essentially west to the Pacific Ocean. Moreover, large mountain glaciers formed in the Rockies, the Cascades and the Sierra Nevada Mountains down to Southern California. Glaciations in Wisconsin were unusual, because the southwestern area of the State was never glaciated, that region always by-passed by all the advancing glaciers. See figure 23.

Rock debris penetrates the ice of an advancing glacier. Therefore, where glaciers contact bedrock, with rocks embedded in the ice acting as chisels, moving glaciers produce scratches and grooves in the bedrock. This scouring of bedrock is called "stria." Scouring creates even more debris, adding to the glacial rock load.

The evidence clearly shows that the Glacial Epoch oscillated, that is, partially melted and advanced, and each time it advanced it usually obliterated, or pushed, or even slid over the voluminous rock debris ("till") previously produced. (However, sometimes enough time transpired between a retreat and an advance for a soil to form on the previous till, which soil often supported the growth of trees. See figure 24 and footnote one. Subsequent glacial advances usually obliterated such growths. Therefore, finding vegetation as shown in figure 24 is unusual.) As a result, those repetitious advances, like plows, piled up "terminal moraines" at the glacier's furthest advance. Moraines, a disorganized jumble of moderate hills were, of course, a conglomeration of all kinds of boulders, rocks, gravel and sand. In the process of advancing, melting, advancing, melting, and advancing again, the glaciers created an extensive array of phenomena, such as drumlins, kames, eskers, kettles, stria, and varves. Chart 2 explains several of these phenomena.

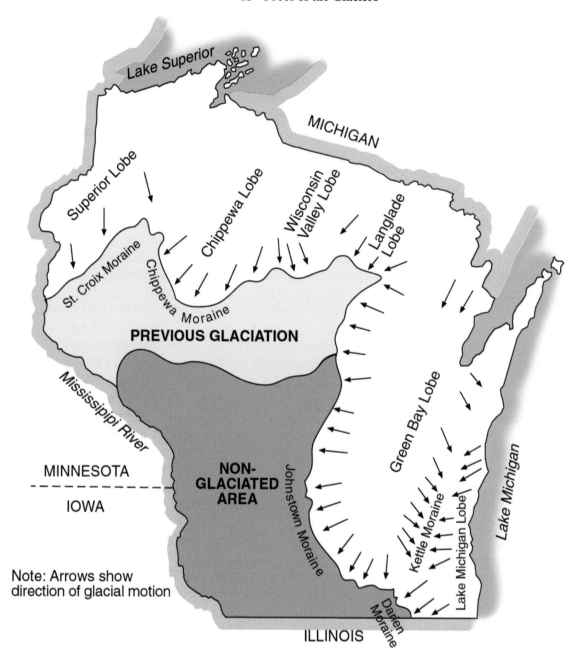

Wisconsin Phase, Glacial Epoch in Wisconsin
Figure 23

(More than half of Canada, from its northern and eastern coasts and almost to its southern borders and far into its western plains, was almost completely stripped of top soil. That vast area was wiped clean by the massive glacial dome that covered it. All that remains in those regions are, primarily, striated and polished granite and strata leaving almost no soil. Most of the rock that was removed from Canada became the abundant

Interglacial buried vegetation, Two Creeks, Wisconsin
Figure 24

till that was deposited in the Northern United States. That till became the source of the phenomena listed above and described below.)

Figure 23 diagrams the Green Bay Lobe of the Wisconsin Phase, one lobe of many of the glacier's final advance. Terminal moraines outline the Green Bay lobe's last advance and its final resting place. Within that lobe's final resting area are thousands of "drumlins." These long, smooth and tapering hills always line up in the direction the ice moved. See figure 25 and footnote 2. That is, the Green Bay glacier slid over the abundant till that had been made by the previous phases and, in the process of sliding, the glacier formed drumlins. Drumlins are usually steeper on the glacier's on-coming side and taper off on its out-going side. A drumlin looks like a very elongated, streamlined teardrop. Because they line up with the direction of glacial movement, drumlins near the moraines point directly at the terminal moraine the advancing glacier was making in that area.[3] Wherever the ground cover between drumlins is thin enough so that bedrock can be examined, the directions of the drumlins and the stria on the bedrock always point in the same direction.. See figure 26 and footnote 4.

Almost always, drumlins contain nothing but completely unsorted rocks, gravel, and sand. (This lack of sorting reveals that moving water did not form them.) This unsorted structure means that a drumlin's smooth, elongated shape and direction were determined only by the moving glacier above it, that is, by the pressures of the glacier. What an expression of the movements and the magnitude of the glaciers and the extensive debris the glaciers produced!

Drumlins, southwest end, Green Bay Lobe
Figure 25 *Turn page 90°*

Stria on limestone bedrock, Madison, Wisconsin
Figure 26

Wherever glaciers were active, stria are found. (Stria and polished bedrock are found in Central Park of New York City, just off Fifth Avenue and 102nd, and just off Central Park West and 63rd.) Concerning drumlins, it is a marvelous sight from an airplane to look down on southern Wisconsin to see the thousands of drumlins fanning out across the State, and even to see the subtle changes in the directions made by the moving glacier.

Figure 27 shows one possible indicator for dating the demise of the Ice Age. As the glaciers were melting, many lakes formed at the edges of the glaciers. These lakes received the melt waters coming from under the ice. Now, glacial rivers contain "rock flour" (also call "glacial milk"), the results of rocks grinding rocks. In the summer, the glaciers melted more, while in the winter they melted less, and in the winter those glacial Lakes were frozen over. As a result, in the summer, with more melting, the rock flour produced thicker and coarser sediments on the lake bottoms, while in winter, with colder and calmer conditions, the deposits were less and were finer in texture.[5] The winter deposits tend to be darker and richer in color. The varves over-all color was determined by the color of the bedrock the glacier had been eroding.

Varves, central area, Green Bay Lobe
Figure 27

After the glacier had melted far away, this sequence of summer-winter deposits left behind banded clay layers in the lakebeds now dry. These clay layers are called "varves." These clay layers are annual indicators. Because of climate variations, statistically linking the summer-winter dimensions of the layers in one dry lake to the corresponding dimensions in next dry lake to the north, and thereby following the retreating glacier's melting sequences, a valid count can often be made for dating how long it took the glacier to disappear from that region.[6]

The picture of varves shown in figure 27 was taken about 60 miles southwest of Green Bay, Wisconsin. The rock flour that made these clay layers came from the melting Green Bay Lobe. Notice near the center, under the leaves and branches, the spring water running over the clay layers. The denser, darker, thinner, winter layers, being more resistive to erosion from the running water, protrude. This varve exposure shows a sequence of over 20 years of rock-flour accumulation. A brick factory, using this clay, was nearby.

Chart 2

In addition to moraines, drumlins, stria, and varves, the melting glaciers produced other significant formations:

Eskers: Formed by rivers that made tunnels in the ice along the bottom of the glacier. When the glacier melted away, the water-sorted gravel and sand that was in these inverted tunnels left winding ridges, some snaking miles long and many tens of feet high.

Kettles: Formed when large blocks of ice broke off, were forced down and buried in the glacial till below, remaining there long after the main glacial body had melted away. Slowly melting, these buried blocks of ice left steep-sided depressions that look like cooking kettles. Today they often form small lakes or flat marshes surrounded by steep hill sides.

Kames: Many were formed by glacial surface rivers that eventually penetrated the glacier, carrying rocks and gravel down to the bottom of the glacier to form cone shaped hills of till.

Erratic Boulders: Very large rocks, usually sitting alone, that are completely dissimilar to any of the local bedrocks. Usually igneous, their rock characteristics can often be traced to igneous bedrock that exists hundreds of miles away. These rocks were broken off, lifted up, and carried far away by the moving glacier.

These phenomena exist along the furthest advances of continental glaciers. The results of the Glacial Epoch are probably the best established of all geologic phenomena. Observing glacial remains is like observing living history.

(The following two subjects are relevant to the Glacial Epoch: (1) Mankind, the human races of, e.g. Neanderthal and Cro-Magnon, lived in Europe during the Ice Age and survived along the southern edges of the glaciers. In their caves and rock shelters and on their artifacts they drew beautiful pictures of cold weather animals, such as mammoths, woolly rhinoceros, bison, and herds of reindeer. In these caves and shelters are their graves, tools, weapons, cultural artifacts, and the bones of these same animals, the remains of what the people ate. (2) The climate in Northern Africa was wetter during the Glacial Epoch. The Sahara had water and supported abundant life. Close by, Abraham's world, though later than Peleg's world, may not have been very dry.)

The Southern Ice Mass

The following section establishes that "the earth was divided" during the Glacial Epoch.

A common assertion in secular geology is that during the Pleistocene, three times more ice formed in the Northern Hemisphere than in the Southern Hemisphere. This assertion of the Pleistocene's southern glacial size is based on the location of the southern continents as they are today. The secular theory is that for many millions of years, Antarctica was and still is the only significant continent in the southern hemisphere where glaciers could form. With that theory, their assertion is logical. However, that assertion is, clearly, not correct. The evidence shows that the southern ice mass of the Pleistocene was probably as big if not bigger than the northern ice mass. The evidence behind this correction of the secular theory is as follows:

Apart from glacial evidence, geologic and biologic evidence reveal that South America, Africa, India, and Australia, were once joined with the continent of Antarctica, and these connected lands constituted the southern part of the undivided Pangaea. Figure 1 describes the approximate southern geography of Pangaea before it divided.[7] The secular dating of this unified, Pangaean arrangement is the late Paleozoic Era, that is, the period about 250 million years ago.[8] Then, according to the secular sequence, following the Paleozoic Era, Pangaea began to divide which, of course, brought an end to the possibility of a development of a very large ice mass in the southern hemisphere. This division theory is the basis of the secular assertion that the Pleistocene's glaciers were three times larger in the north than in the south.

According to secular theory, in the Paleozoic Era, a very large glacier existed on Southern Pangaea before Pangaea divided. Glacial remains, such as stria, and other glacial phenomena, including drumlins and erratic boulders, are found in the southeastern fourth of South America, throughout the southern half of Africa,[9] the southern half of India, and the southern third of Australia. When the glacial evidence, especially the directions of the stria, are connected together, the evidence reveals that a great ice mass existed on Southern Pangaea. It extended far out from Antarctica into the four landmasses listed above. In other words, according to secular reasoning, a great glacier existed on the southern portion of Pangaea during the Paleozoic. Obviously, secular geology considers this a "Paleozoic" glacial epoch as distinct from the Pleistocene Glacial Epoch. (We have been calling the Pleistocene *the* "Glacial Epoch.") What is the secular rationale? They "know" when Pangaea existed, when all these lands were together and were able to support such a massive glacial accumulation and, with their time scale, to explain the glacial evidence. Therefore, in their estimation, this Paleozoic glacial epoch could only have existed when Pangaea existed, that is, during the Paleozoic, and not later.

A glaring inconsistency is involved in this secular theory concerning a Paleozoic glacial epoch. According to their theory, the Paleozoic glacial epoch existed only in the southern portion of Pangaea. That is, a corresponding northern ice mass did not exist at that time. "In contrast [to the southern ice mass], the present-day continents in the Northern Hemisphere show no trace of glaciations during this time."[10] It is extremely unlikely that an immense glacial mass existed only in the southern hemisphere and not in the northern hemisphere at that same time. If there had been an abundance of snowfall in the south to create the southern ice mass, there should have been abundance in the north as well. Secular geology should recognize that there is something fundamentally wrong with their theory.

For our apologetic purposes, we need to verify that a very large ice mass did exist on Southern Pangaea. It is important that we carefully examine the stria evidence that

Stria, coming toward viewer, Southern Australia
Figure 28

Stria, Southern Africa
Figure 29

69

show the directions of movement and the extent of that large glacier. (As examples of the stria, see figures 28 and 29.)[11] The movements of that southern glacier are revealing.[12] Examining the stria on these four continents, we find the evidence compelling: In all areas except the southwest coast of Africa, the stria movement is away from the oceans. Those directions are significant! *Glaciers do not develop over oceans*. Rather, glaciers move toward oceans. *Glaciers develop over land*. Examine the directions in figure 30. Those directions reveal that these five land masses were once joined, and the large glacier producing those stria directions had a center located on the connected land that *became* Antarctica and Southwestern Africa and from that center the glacier moved outward into the lands that *became* South America, Northern and Eastern Africa, India, and Australia. See figure 31. (Very revealing stria exists along the southern coast of Australia: Leaving the water's edge are stria on the shoreline's bedrock. This stria reveals that land existed where the Indian Ocean is today. This is excellent evidence of Pangaea before it separated.[13]) That is, with the evidence of the stria (and other supporting non-glacial geologic evidence) this connected Pangaean land arrangement is the only arrangement that explains the southern glacier's existence, its movements and its boundaries. *Indeed, a great ice mass once covered southern Pangaea.*

The secular dating of this southern ice mass is based on the secular dating of Pangaea. However, if Pangaea existed in Peleg's day, and not 250 million years ago, the glacial evidence reveals that that southern ice mass existed at the same time as the northern ice mass of the Pleistocene and was very large and possibly larger than the northern ice mass. That is, the two glacial masses existed at the same time. Only this explanation makes sense. The evidence is clear that a Paleozoic glacial epoch never existed! That southern ice mass was a Pleistocene ice mass – and it was big.

Shifting our attention to the north, the secular theory concerning the Pleistocene in the Northern Hemisphere has another problem. According to that theory, the glaciers that encroached on the northern regions of North America, Europe, and Asia did so with the Artic Ocean and the North Atlantic Ocean right in the middle of those glaciers. That those separate, continental glacial masses would have developed without North America, Europe, and Asia being joined as the southern lands of Pangaea were joined, would have been highly improbable. (With the present continental arrangements, the development of the much smaller European and Asian glaciers would have been highly unlikely; some of those non-mountainous, continental glaciers were very small.) Glaciers do not develop over oceans! Rather, the northern ice mass had an origin like the origin of the southern ice mass. That is, a connected northern Pangaean surface existed (connecting North America, Europe, and Asia) enabling that massive glacier to develop. The northern glacier grew, as the southern glacier grew, until Pangaea divided, *after* which the Artic and the Atlantic Oceans opened and developed.

Furthermore, glacial evidence on the floor of the Artic Ocean indicates that the Artic opened and developed during the Glacial Epoch. The sea-bottom evidence indicates that as Pangaea was separating and the Artic Ocean was opening, some of the immense glaciers that were above it were forced into the developing Artic Ocean. These glaciers, with their load of rocks, dug deep and long channels in the ocean floor, channels that today are over 600 miles from the nearest land. Secular geology, with its present

Southern Ice Mass evidence after Pangaea's Division
Figure 30

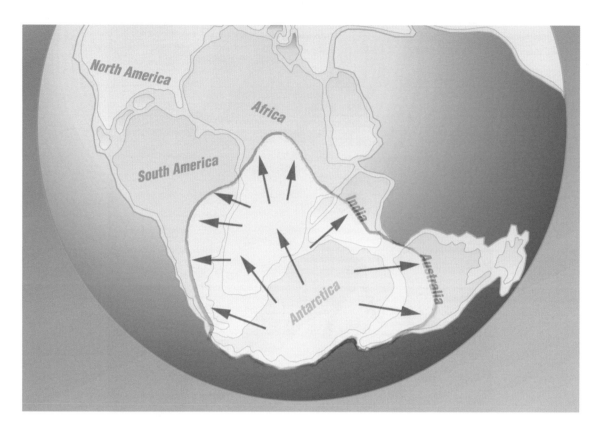

The Southern Ice Mass reconstructed, before division
Figure 31

distribution of the continents, cannot explain how glaciers produced such channels so far from land.[14] Similar phenomena exist in the oceans around Antarctica. Glacial remains (see the chart below) occur more than 135 miles from the present limits of that continent.[15] These remains indicate that the glaciers from Pangaea were still effective as the continents around Antarctica were pulling away from Antarctica..

To express our thesis geographically, the physical locations of the two glaciers on undivided Pangaea during the Ice Age, a diagram like Figure 31 needs to be developed for the glaciers of Northern Pangaea at the height of the Pleistocene. Secular geology developed figure 31. But secular geology could not and would not develop the northern Pleistocene geography we need. To develop such a diagram would be impossible for them, because they maintain that their Pangaean and Pleistocene times were separated by at least 200 million years.

Figure 32 is our attempt to complete the young earth picture of our Pangaea with its two massive glaciers at the height of the Glacial Epoch. The boundaries of the Southern Ice Mass are based on the geography of figure 31. The boundaries of the Northern Ice Mass are based on the geography given by figure 22, with modifications to reflect the pending openings of the Artic and Atlantic oceans. (The far northern approximation of its glacier shown in figure 32 is not very accurate.)

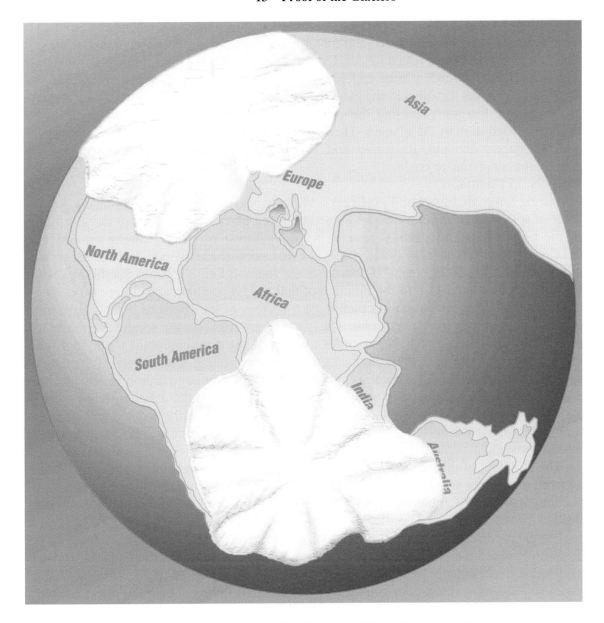

The Glacial Epoch's Northern and Southern Ice Masses
Figure 32

In summary, the geography of the southern ice mass reveals an important truth: The glacial remains in South America, Africa, India, and Australia, as well as Antarctica, demonstrate clearly that these lands existed together as one landmass, and then, during the Pleistocene, Pangaea divided into the continents of today. (The glacial remains of the Northern Hemisphere reveal the same truth.) This is the message of this book: *The division of Pangaea, the days of Peleg when "the earth was divided," occurred during the Glacial Epoch.*

Finally, the massive glaciers in Northern and Southern Pangaea were like two very large trucks picking up speed and traveling in opposite directions on one-way streets that had no stop signs. Because of feedback mechanisms, once underway the two continental glaciers tended to be self-perpetuating and increasing.[16] Apparently, only the division of Pangaea terminated the glaciers' growth. Pangaea's division took the fuel out of the factors that were causing the prodigious snowfalls and brought changes in the climate needed to melt the glaciers. However, the Glacial Epoch did last for many years after Pangaea's division. Its forces and stresses were still effective, and some of its effectiveness remains today.[17]

Chapter 13 Footnotes

1 – Along Lake Michigan, at Two Creeks, Wisconsin, 17 miles north of Manitowoc, is a layer of soil with vegetation that developed between glacial phases. There the glacial till of the Green Bay Lobe gently covered a young forest of trees growing on soil that developed on previous glacial till. The trees that grew there averaged 60 years of age, with some as old as 120 years: Wisconsin State Journal, Feb 28, 1968. See figure 24. In Chernicoff et al, see page 544 for a picture of that soil, vegetation, and cover of till.

2 - Figure 25 is an early morning picture of a portion of the southern 2000 square mile drumlin field of the Green Bay Lobe. The glacier here was moving southwest. (Note the fence lines indicating east.) Twenty miles to the east the drumlins point south, and forty miles east the drumlins point southeast, all revealing the glacier's spreading motion. Note the many small, subtle drumlins and the village built on large drumlins.

3 - The continual smoothness of adjacent drumlins throughout the drumlin field indicates that the glacier's motion was continuous – until the glacier finally stopped and began to melt. This phenomenon indicates that continuous glacial advances over long distances were steady and accomplished in a short time. See figure 25.

4 - The direction of this stria and the neighboring drumlins is the same. **Note**: the till that covered this stria was contemporaneous with the stria – they were not sequential.

5 - Some particles of winter rock flour were so fine that many days and calm waters were needed for those particles to settle.

6 - For the procedures of varve dating up the Connecticut River Valley see, Antevs.

7 - With Pangaea's division, Africa and India moved north, bringing some glacial remains even north of the equator. Australia also moved north.

8 - In "B.C." terms, the secular geologic time scale, in millions of years, is approximately as follows: the Paleozoic ("old life") Era goes from 550 to 250; the Mesozoic ("middle life") Era goes from 250 to 65; and the Cenozoic ("new life") Era goes from 65 to the present.

9 - Stria and drumlins exist in the Southern Sahara. Nature, Sept. 15, 2005, 299.

10 - Hamblin et al, 465.

11 - Figure 28 illustrates a significant issue: Behind the people is terrain covering the same surface of stria upon which the two are standing. Even if stria is covered, a careful examination will undoubtedly show that those coverings are not "old" such as a supposed "Paleozoic" covering, but are a Pleistocene covering, contemporaneous with the stria, or even younger. See footnotes, 4, 9 and the appendix article, Further Research.

12 - Determining glacial motion is done by examining the "scouring" and "plucking" characteristics of the stria. Scouring (also called abrasion) is due to chiseling, while plucking is due to isolation and removal of surface weaknesses by temporary freezing.

13 - See Figure 12.13 in Plummer, et al.

14 - "Enigmatic Artic ice sheets Science": Aug 5, 1994, 735; Nature, Mar 22, 2001, 427; Science News, Mar 24, 2001, 181.

15 - Science, Oct 15, 2004, 403.

16 - Snow and cold, especially when the two together form large ice sheets, tend to perpetuate themselves. The ice sheets augment snowfall by chilling the air. The ice sheets inhibit the summer heat from warming the air, because the sun's heat is consumed in melting ice. Finally, the snow reflects sunlight back into space and therefore lessens the absorption of the sun's energy. Other factors work to perpetuate and grow large ice sheets.

17 - Research is needed to determine why the Glacial Epoch had periods of melting and advancing.

14 - Earthquakes Today

We live in an unstable world, and it probably will become increasingly unstable. The Word tells us that instabilities of every kind, social, political, moral, spiritual, and physical, are to come "before the great and awesome Day of the Lord comes." (Joel 2, Hag 2, Mat 24, Mk 13, Lk 21, 2 Thess 2, 1 Tim 4, 2 Tim 3, Rev 6, etc.) The subject of this book has been the earth movements of the past. However, some of the forces that existed in the past are still with us. We need to examine these forces. But before applying them and determining the potentials for earthquakes and volcanoes today, we need briefly to review the history of earth's instabilities.

The Word clearly implies that the earth's instabilities began with the Flood. The original creation and Pangaea were beautiful and obviously very peaceful. It could not have been otherwise. Finally, God brought judgment on a corrupt world. Besides the rain, God used "all the sources of the watery depths." These "burst open" (Gen 7:11). This means that God used crustal upheavals to inundate Pangaea. (For this flooding factor, see footnote 1 of chapter 3.) Consequently, with the Flood, Pangaea and the ocean floor ceased to be tranquil.

When God brought the Flood year to an end, "the fountains of the deep…were closed" (Gen 8:2). Thus, God caused extreme seismic upheavals to cease. Apparently, however, God never allowed the earth to return to its pre-Flood tranquility. The earth was now stressed. The Scriptures describe a world after the Flood as having climatic, seismic, and other physical vicissitudes. Life was not easy. That is exactly what God wants - that we do not look for utopia here. Until the End, utopia will not come. God wants us to look forward to His new heavens and His new earth. Therefore, since the Flood, God never caused all global instability to cease. God did end the extreme turmoil of the Flood, but He brought new instabilities to the world: storms, droughts, earthquakes, and volcanoes. Furthermore, God divided the earth in Peleg's day. Reflecting on Peleg's day, those years and the years that followed were, obviously, subject to many severe earthquakes and volcanism. We should be thankful that, as the continents slowed their movements, the severity of those earthquakes and extrusions have diminished. Nevertheless, today's continents are still moving. Though the severities of Peleg's day no longer exist, the forces we have studied do exist. An analogy would be a person who had a severe illness and is now much better but is still not fully recovered. Our earth is still unstable! What are the potentials for an increase in earthquakes today?

The answer will depend in part on the rate at which today's glaciers melt. One simple factor will be the rate of transfer of the north and south vertical loadings, i.e. the release of pressures as the high latitude glaciers melt and the increase of downward pressures on the low latitudes as sea levels rise. This transfer of mass-pressures, rapidly produced, would generate earthquakes and volcanoes. However, the inertial factors produced by glacial melting are more significant and more complex. Let us briefly review the forces and energies that created Peleg's instabilities and then analyze which of these inertial factors are still significant.

First was the force from the conservation of angular momentum due to the movement of water-mass toward the earth's axis of rotation. Second was the reshaping of the earth and the centrifugal force due to the unnatural relocation of mass from its natural low-latitude locations. The third force was precession from the earth seeking to maintain directional stability, which the circling glaciers disturbed.

What were the energies that were stored? Under stress, the crust of the earth stored elastic potential energy. Heat was generated because of the strains that the stresses produced. Then the great glaciers stored gravitational, positional, and rotational energies. Other energies may have been generated.

This then summarizes the primary forces and energies existing in Peleg's day. Which of these are important today? We have the remnants of the Glacial Epoch with us. Our earth has adjusted fairly well to our two large glacial masses. But this is where our present difficulties begin. The glacial remains to which our earth had adjusted are not remaining the same. They are melting. Global warming appears to be a fact. Almost all glaciers worldwide are shrinking significantly. The rise in sea levels causing coastal damage are concerns. However, of immediate concern are the instabilities that glacial melting are producing.

Today the earth has about 160,000 glaciers.[1] The evidence is that almost all of them are disappearing.[2] Therefore, the waters in those glaciers are no longer in fixed positions, but their waters are free to move. Furthermore, most glaciers are located in the higher latitudes and therefore are nearer the earth's rotation axis. This situation is exactly the reverse of the Ice Age buildup and its effects, for example, on the earth's angular momentum. This momentum effect from melting is working to slow the earth's rotation rather than speeding it up.[3] Melting is creating other inertial dynamics. These phenomena are gradual and therefore the stress buildup is gradual. It is a buildup of stress never the less. Moreover, stresses produce earthquakes. Furthermore, with global warming, the melting of these many glaciers may accelerate which, of course would accelerate stresses.

The melting of the glaciers on Antarctica and Greenland, where most of the earth's ice is stored, is critical. See figure 33. The same principles and processes we described apply to them. Melting their glaciers would be more significant in terms of stress, energy, and instability. Concerning Antarctica, sections as large as some of our small States are in melting conditions where they might disconnect and move into the ocean. Grounded ice sheets are blocking many of Antarctica's glaciers from the sea. However, melting is removing those blocks, thus providing exist routes for the glaciers. When that happens, a glacier's movement into the sea could quickly change the earth's rotational dynamics, e.g. by rising sea levels and by removing the glacier's land connections. These sequences could generate stressful conditions.[4]

When all the earth's many small glaciers were being formed, energy was stored in various ways. The specific storage for each glacier was, individually, complex. How those energies will be released as the glaciers melt would be a challenge to unravel. However, Antarctica is a clearer issue. The energy storage of Antarctica is very great. Because the center of gravity of Antarctica's glaciers may be close to the earth's axis, the precession stresses produced by their melting may be small. However, Antarctica's rotational energy, and the crust's elastic potential energy due to momentum and centrifugal forces must be great. In any case, the melting and movement of Antarctica's

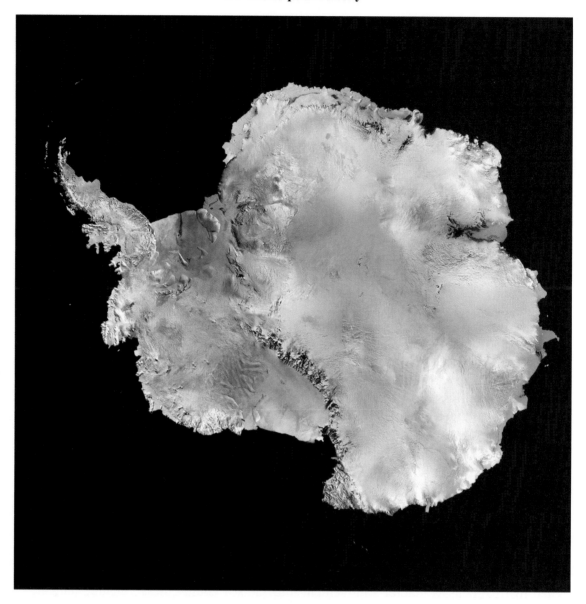

Antarctica, one-tenth of Earth's land surface
Figure 33

glaciers, and all the other glaciers, must release their various energies. This release must affect the stresses in the earth's crust.

One possible critical situation is as follows: If, over many years the immense masses of Antarctica moved down and are now floating, the earth would have had time, partially, to adjust. However, if some of the masses are not floating, and if the elevated ice becomes detached and rapidly moves into the sea, the effects could be serious. First, globally, the sea levels, especially the equatorial waters would rise slightly but rapidly. Because the earth would conserve its angular momentum, this increase in the earth's equatorial mass, with its greater radii, would work, even slightly, to slow the earth's rotation - or the crust would try to - while the "big earth" below would want to keep on rotating.

This sequence is exactly opposite to the glacial buildup of the Ice Age. The significant difference is not just the new direction, that is, the "build-down," but it is in the timing: The Ice Age buildup was over many years. Moving a large Antarctica section into the sea in only days would create a rapid change in the earth's rotation - or try to. That is, the Ice Age buildup gradually demanded a speed up in the earth's rotation. However, a large change would generate a sudden demand to slow the earth's rotation. In addition, by floating, the glaciers' fixed physical connections to the earth would suddenly cease. This braking action would create significant stresses in the earth's crust. Furthermore, sudden increases in the water's vertical loading on the equatorial crust and decreases in the loading on the polar crust would also produce stresses.

Stresses are the cause of earthquakes. Therefore, more earthquakes or stronger earthquakes and new eruptions will probably result. What we have described thus far is sufficient to show that we should not be surprised if more earthquakes occur.

No matter what happens, we can take comfort in God's promise: "Therefore, we will not fear though the earth gives way, though the mountains be moved into the heart of the sea, though its waters roar and foam, though the mountains tremble at its swelling." (Ps 46:2-3)

Chapter 14 Footnotes

1 - Science, Nov 26, 2004, 1441.

2 - Nature, Nov 17, 2005, 275.

3 - "Because glacial melting redistributes Earth's mass from high latitudes, where water is stored as ice, to lower latitudes, any appreciable melting should change the planet's rate of rotation…." Science, April 7, 2006.

The following fact is significant: The earth's rotation is slowing. Our clocks are approximately 0.4 milliseconds per day faster than the earth's day. Therefore, to keep our clocks in sync with the slowing earth, it is necessary to add a second to our clocks periodically. A second was added at the beginning of 2006. The previous addition was in 1999. Because of the inertia of the earth's core and mantle, the "big-earth," and its desire to keep rotating at the same rate, the braking action through the crust that slows the earth's rotation rate creates heat in the asthenosphere and stresses in the earth's lithosphere. These stresses produce earthquakes and the heat produces volcanoes.

4 - Science, Oct 8, 2004, 193, 255.

"The possibility that the West Antarctica Ice Sheet will collapse….is of concern, because such an event would imply a sudden increase in sea level."
Science, Mar 7, 2003, 1560.

"The latest gauging of West Antarctica glaciers confirms that when the ocean eats at one end of a glacier, it can draw far-distant ice toward the sea, with potentially dangerous consequences." Science, Sept 24, 2004, 1897.

15 – Radiometrics

Secular geology dates the division of Pangaea to about two hundred and fifty million years ago, and dates the Glacial Epoch, the Pleistocene, to many thousands of years ago. These dates are primarily determined by three related time measurements: the uniformitarian theory of geology and the Theory of Evolution (which are, essentially, philosophical world views), and the dating measurements of radiometrics.

Radiometrics is a time measurement method based on the phenomena of atomic decay. Radioactive atoms are unstable and partially "come apart." That is, these atoms give up parts of themselves, such as an electron or proton or neutron. (Radioactive atoms decay in a random manner, some quicker than others. Because measurements involve innumerable numbers of atoms, it is the average decay rate that is significant.) As they decay, these radioactive atoms lose mass and become simpler. Ultimately, they become non-radioactive; in becoming simpler they finally stop decaying. Concerning the terminology used in radiometrics, the original atom, the atom at the beginning of its decay process, is called the "parent" atom, and the associated non-radioactive atom at the end of the decay process is called the "daughter" atom.

Decay rates can be measured. The average rate is expressed as its "half-life." For example, assume a material initially containing only parent atoms. After some time of decaying randomly, one-half of those atoms will have become daughter atoms. That length of time is called that atom's half-life. Apply these principles to an example: Assume dating a rock containing atoms whose half-life is 10,000 years. In the lab, measurements determine that the rock contains one gram of parent atoms and one gram of daughter atoms. Therefore, we may reason, the age of the rock must be 10,000 years.

However, note the assumptions in this reasoning: (1) the rock had no daughter atoms when those parent atoms began their decay process; (2) the atoms' rate of decay did not change during those 10,000 years; and (3) no parent or daughter atoms were added or taken away, that is, no additions or subtractions (leaching) of the rock occurred during those 10,000 years. That is, that rock was sealed from external gains or losses.

All three assumptions are significant. The sealed requirement of the third assumption is usually very difficult to meet. However, it is a necessary condition to get a valid measurement. The rate requirement of the second assumption is the condition most likely to be met. Decay rates are usually very constant and are not easily altered by external forces. The first assumption, concerning the absence of daughter atoms in the rock at the beginning of the decay sequence is crucial. For if daughter atoms were in that rock 10,00 years ago, that dating reasoning would not be valid.

It is the first assumption (no daughter atoms in the original material) that is most affected by the worldview of Evolution. Evolution negates the possibility of the rapid creation of a functioning world, a world with trees, soil, rocks with all their minerals, a supportive environment with "apparent age," not real age, into which God placed Adam and Eve. God created Adam and Eve with apparent age. The trees had apparent age. The soil had apparent age. Everything that God commanded into existence had apparent age. That is what God's original creation was all about. It did not evolve. God created it to function immediately. The Creation began with apparent age.

The phenomenon of apparent age applies to radiometric's first assumption, that is, the initial conditions of the material to be measured. Consider this example: One useful atom, lead (Pb206), is a non-radioactive daughter atom of the very long decay sequence of the radioactive parent atom, uranium (U238). Did not some of the rocks of Adam and Eve's world contain this useful atom, lead? If the rocks did contain this lead, and some uranium, secular lab tests would have declared those rocks, containing the uranium and lead, to be very old.[1] However, they were not very old; they were only days old. Only an evolutionary worldview, which denies the creation of a functioning world, would declare the rocks to be old. Secular geology's worldview, with its assumptions, often affects their dating results. Their radiometric measurements often give dates of, supposedly, millions and billions of years. Furthermore, the measurements that totally disagree with their assumptions are considered "spurious" and therefore are rejected.

The issues in uranium-lead dating are more involved than those given in the above description. Moreover, other radioactive and non-radioactive measurement methods exist.[2] It is not necessary or appropriate to examine all those details here. The summary above covers the essential issues.

One radiometric measurement that can be valuable to Believers are those made with radioactive carbon, carbon 14 (^{14}C). ^{14}C measurements can be valid. In addition, even with its short half-life, new ^{14}C measurements are negating the long-age assertions of secular geology and of Evolution. We will now explain this new powerful evidence.

A little background is necessary to understand the ^{14}C measuring process: A ^{14}C atom is created in the atmosphere when a neutron from outer space penetrates a nitrogen atom. If the nitrogen atom absorbs the neutron, it becomes a ^{14}C atom. (Natural carbon is ^{12}C.) However, because the natural state of ^{14}C is nitrogen, ^{14}C is unstable. In time it reverts (decays) to its original nitrogen state. ^{14}C half-life is 5730 years. However, as long as it exists as a carbon atom, ^{14}C acts chemically like a natural ^{12}C atom. That is, ^{14}C also becomes part of all life supporting, carbon-containing molecules. Thus, ^{14}C becomes part of living trees, animals, humans, etc. As long as the trees, animals, and humans are living, like all the other carbon atoms in their bodies, ^{14}C is dynamically interchanged with the atmosphere, which of course also has ^{14}C atoms. Therefore, the ^{14}C level in the living creature remains constant; the creature takes in as much ^{14}C as it gives out. However, once the living form dies, that dynamic interchange stops. Once it stops, the level of ^{14}C in that dead form cannot remain the same, because ^{14}C is always in the decay process back to its normal nitrogen state. Therefore, knowing the half-life of ^{14}C, by measuring the level of ^{14}C remaining in the dead form, the age of that form can be determined.

The same three assumptions we have discussed above also apply to ^{14}C dating. The first assumption is the most important. That is, what was the level of ^{14}C in the atmosphere when the form was living? Was it the same as today? Or, was less ^{14}C being produced at that time? If there were less ^{14}C at that time, then measuring the dead form's ^{14}C level today would indicate that that form of life was more ancient than it really is.

Obviously, knowing the production of ^{14}C in the atmosphere in the past is very important in order to obtain valid dating. Experience has shown that ^{14}C dating of dead forms that are not too old tend to be quite accurate. We are able to compare ^{14}C dates with dates known by other means, such as the mummies in the pyramids of Egypt, whose burial dates are known, or the date of an historic wood artifact, or a wood beam in some known archeological site. [14]C dates can be compared with known historical dates. However, ^{14}C dating errors generally increase the further back in time the dating goes.[3]

The following discussion outlines a very important development. Significant sensitivity improvements in ^{14}C detection, and the successful removal of essentially all atmospheric ^{14}C contamination, have now enabled the detection of ^{14}C in many coal layers.[4] If those coals were as old as secular geology maintains they are (e.g. many millions of years old), those coals should be ^{14}C dead. However, those coals are still ^{14}C alive! The ^{14}C presence shows that the coal layers are only thousands of years old, not millions. Furthermore, ^{14}C is now detected in many organic forms (oil, gas, and many other fossils with carbon contents) that are declared by secular geology to be very old.

More significantly, the ^{14}C dating of all these "old" organic fossils usually give approximately the same age no matter where the fossils occur in the stratigraphic record. That is, fossils containing carbon that are found at the bottom of the sedimentary record – supposedly the oldest – give, in general, the same ^{14}C age as those fossils found in the top sediments which, being at the top were, supposedly, the youngest. These phenomena contradict the secular claim that it took many millions of years to develop the entire stratigraphic record. This new ^{14}C dating indicates that all these fossils were forms that were alive at the same time and were all buried at the same time. These results are a challenge to the supposed long ages it took to make the stratigraphic record but are a support for the older catastrophic interpretation. (See chapter 2.) These ^{14}C measurements are a strong support for the reality of the Flood of Genesis. Moreover, these ^{14}C phenomena disprove the supposed long ages that it took to divide Pangaea.

Even more important is this truth: The uniformitarian theory for the gradual development of the sedimentary rock record made possible the Theory of Evolution. If the sedimentary rocks were formed quickly, the basic (fossil) "proof" for the Theory of Evolution has been destroyed; the time needed for the evolutionary process is gone.

Chapter 15 Footnotes

1 - Uranium 238 decays to Lead 206 in a series of 14 emissions in which 10 protons, 22 neutrons, and 10 electrons are lost. The numbers, 238 and 206, are those atom's approximate weights relative to hydrogen's weight of one. From these weights, we see that during the decay of the parent atom, uranium, to the daughter atom, lead, 32 units of mass were emitted. (238 minus 206 equal 32. Like the hydrogen atom, a proton and a neutron both have atomic weights of essentially one. An electron is almost weightless.) Thus, 10 protons plus 22 neutrons equals 32 units of mass. These 32 units were emitted in the decay process.

The normal half-life of this long, uranium-to-lead emission sequence is 4.5 billion years. Techniques exist for measuring this long half-life.

2 - The following are two radioactive relationships frequently used in radiometrics: (1) the parent atom, Potassium-40 decaying to the daughter atom, Argon-40, with a half-life of 1.3 billion years, and (2) the parent atom, Rubidium-87, decaying to the daughter atom, Strontium-87, with a half-life of 49 billion years. Also non-radioactive dating techniques exist, such as thermoluminescence, in which crystal grains are heated to force out the sunlight energy the grains stored over time.

3 - The production of ^{14}C in the atmosphere has varied. "To know the true age of a carbon-containing sample, one must know the initial amount of ^{14}C at time zero." Science, Nov 30, 2001, 1844. Recognizing this fact, secular geologists are seeking to make their ^{14}C dating more accurate by "calibrating" their results so that they agree with the dates done by other means. It is good that they recognize the ^{14}C production variability of the past. However, secular geologists make their dates agree with the Theory of Evolution. This is predisposed reasoning. Science, Jan 9, 2004, 178, 202; Jan. 21, 2005, 362; June 10, 2005, 1551.

4 - 5th ICC, 2003, 127-142.

16 - Evidence For A Young World

This chapter gives additional evidence that the world, and life, is much younger than the millions and billions of years of evolutionary theory. If the earth is young, the secular theories concerning the time of Pangaea's division, and the Theory of Evolution, are not valid. More data could be given.[1] Old earth theories are also briefly summarized.

1. Spiral galaxies consist of millions of stars rotating around a galactic center. The stars closest to the center rotate faster than the stars further out. If the galaxies were hundreds of millions of years old, we would no longer see spiral arms. Because of the difference in rotation rates, we would see a featureless disc of stars. However, we still see spiral arms.

2. A supernova is the result of an exploding star, which explosion remains visible, for example, a million years. Statistics indicate that supernovas in a galaxy occur on the average of one every twenty-five years. However, in our galaxy (the Milky Way galaxy) we observe only about 200 supernovas, not 40,000. This observation indicates that our galaxy is not one million years old – at a million years we should see 40,000 - but is consistent with a young galaxy.

3. Every time a comet orbits the sun, the sun's solar radiation blows matter off the surface of the comet. (Blown-off matter creates the comet's tail, which the sunlight illuminates. Of course, the tail always points away from the sun.) Therefore, because it loses matter from the pressure of the solar radiation, the comet becomes smaller with each orbit of the sun. Therefore, comets have a limited life span, no more, at best, than 100,000 years. To explain the existence of comets in the solar system supposedly 4.6 billion years old, evolutionists propose that an "Oort Cloud," far outside the solar system – which cannot be seen and is proposed only on faith – is the source for new comets. A "Kuiper Belt," on the edge of the solar system, which can be seen, is a suggested source of comets. But without the supply of the Oort Cloud, the Kuiper Belt would have, long ago, been depleted. Secular explanations are based on unsupported theory. Comets are an indication of a young solar system.

4. Meteors are usually metallic rocks (for example, nickel) that come from outer space. Most burn up in the atmosphere creating "shooting stars." Those that land on the earth are called "meteorites." If the stratigraphic fossil record formed over a 600 million year period, those sedimentary rocks should contain many meteorites. However, only a few meteorites have been found in the sediments. This lack of meteorites is a strong indication that the sediments were deposited in a very short time.

5. The sun constantly radiates various forms of matter. As these forms move away from the sun, they "get in the way" of all the objects that are orbiting the sun. "Getting in the way" slows those orbiting objects. An object slowed too much will no longer remain in orbit but will be pulled into the sun. Large objects, such as the earth and the other planets, are slowed very little. However, small objects, such as cosmic dust, are slowed significantly. In time, such small objects, being pulled into the sun, will be removed from the solar system. However, significant amounts of cosmic dust still orbit the sun. This phenomenon indicates that the solar system is young.[2]

6. Prior to the program to land men on the moon, many scientists expressed serious concerns that when the astronauts landed, they and their spacecraft would be buried in a deep layer of lunar dust. Their secular concerns were reasonable. The following reasoning was typical: "Because the moon may be several billion years old, and with the known density of cosmic dust surrounding the moon and the earth (which can be measured), and because the moon has no atmosphere to burn up meteors to stop the constant erosion of the moon's surface, the moon will have accumulated at least a hundred feet of dust." However, the astronauts encountered almost no dust.

The secular concerns about the depth of the dust may have been misplaced: those secular assumptions may not have been valid and that, in fact, dust was never a problem. But, concerning the issue of the depth of dust as a time measurement, "the dust has not yet settled." The lack of dust on the moon may indeed indicate that the moon is young.

7. If the oceans were several billion years old, at the rate that rivers feed the oceans with dissolved elements from the land such as sodium chloride, the oceans should contain much more of these elements, even considering the paths for the removal of these elements from the oceans. The low concentrations in the oceans of these elements indicate that the oceans are young.

8. The existence of large quantities of oil and gas reveals that the sedimentary layers of the earth are very young. The surface of the earth, everywhere, is constantly stressed. (See Chapter 9.) These stresses are constantly fracturing the strata. If the earth's sedimentary rocks were millions of years old, the oil and gas reservoirs in the strata, under high pressure, would have escaped long ago through the fractures. (An example: oil and gas are constantly bubbling up at the Brea Tar Pits in Los Angeles.) Petroleum geologists recognize the release and escape of oil and gas from reservoirs by the continual faulting of the sedimentary rocks. ("Here we use time-lapse…imaging to reveal a pulse of fluid ascending rapidly inside one of these fault zones. Such intermittent fault 'burping' is likely to be an important factor in the migration of subsurface hydrocarbons.")[3] Reservoirs of oil and gas should no longer exist if secular long-age dating were correct.

9. DNA (deoxyribonucleic acid) is a long, elaborate, chemical polymer in the form of a twisted ladder whose "rungs" carry the genetic coding for life. (Mutations are produced, essentially always harmful, when the information carrying rungs are damaged by X-Rays, strong chemicals, etc.) Because of its delicate structure, DNA could not exist in the wild for very long, especially with the presence of water, before the DNA would be degraded. However, scientists have found undamaged DNA in supposedly very old forms, indicating that those forms were not old but young.

10. Soft tissues such as blood vessels, cells and connective tissue have been found in bone fossils supposedly many millions of years old. Those soft tissues should not have survived intact if they were that old. Those tissues indicate a young age.[4]

11. According to the present evolutionary theory, humans (Homo sapiens) have existed for almost 200,000 years. If that were true, several billion skeletons, with their tools and other artifacts should be found. However, only a few thousand skeletons and a minimum of tools and artifacts have been found.

12. The secular anthropologic evidence shows that, over a supposed span of some 200,000 years, Homo sapiens were always very intelligent. Their cultural remains indicate abilities and insights equal to that of modern man. Such intelligent humans should have discovered the arts of writing, the practice of farming, etc. However, such archeological evidence does not exist. The accumulation of all the evidence of human activity contradicts an antiquity of 200,000 years. Rather, the evidence indicates a relatively short human history.

"Old Earth" Theories

Many Believers support one of the following three "Old Earth" theories: (1) the Day-Age theory; (2) the Pre-Adamic Ruin theory (also called the Gap or The Reconstruction theory) and (3) the Theistic Evolution theory.[5] These theories reject the global catastrophism of the Genesis Flood. Therefore, two of these theories require and support long ages to explain the stratigraphic fossil record. In the following brief descriptions, recognize that each theory has other variations.

The Day-Age theory equates the six days of Creation with the secular eras of geologic time. This theory maintains that God created in periods, "ages," that were widely separated in time. These periods correspond approximately to the geologic eras.

The Pre-Adamic Ruin theory usually maintains that in the far distant past, God made a beautiful creation over which Lucifer had authority. When Lucifer sinned, God judged him and destroyed that creation. That judgment produced the stratigraphic record with all its fossils. Then six thousand years ago, God created this present creation, a reconstruction built on the sedimentary remains of that ancient destruction.

The Theistic Evolution theory maintains that God used *survival of the fittest*, tooth and claw, long-age processes of natural selection to create.

These three theories have significant scientific, geologic, Biblical, and theological weaknesses. This book sufficiently addresses these weaknesses, both explicitly and implicitly. However, these old-age theories find strength in the supposedly solid foundation of the great ages indicated by stellar phenomena, the vast stellar distances, indicating a universe millions and billions of years old. If these stellar phenomena and ages are real, they challenge a young world cosmology [study of the universe], and strongly support old-age theories.

Believer's "Solutions"

How do Believers in a young earth seek to explain the stellar evidence? Here are two common approaches to the problem: Most Word honoring Believers regard the creation account of Genesis 1 to be chronologically and literally factual. Most of these Believers maintain that the solar and stellar systems were created on the Fourth Day. Their standard "solution" to the stellar-distance-age problem is that the stellar distances are real but the great ages indicated by them are only apparent. When God called into existence the stellar and solar systems, he created a functioning universe, one that Adam and Eve could immediately see and appreciate. (For a discussion of the phenomena of "apparent age," see chapter 15.) Therefore, on Day 4, God also put the radiant energies from all the stars into their proper places.

However, this explanation has problems: For example, a star, 100,000 light years away, explodes creating a supernova . We see that star exploding today. If thatdid occur, such an event raises ethical and theological problems for the "apparent age" solution of a universe only ten thousand years old: *Has God deceived us*! [6]

Some Word honoring Believers - with the same high regard for the historicity of Genesis 1 - believe that the solar and stellar systems were not created on the Fourth Day, but God had already created them prior to Genesis 1:2a. This second group maintains that *God has not deceived us*. This second "solution" is as follows:

They interpret the past tense of Gen 1:2a ("the earth was") together with Gen 1:1 ("In the beginning God created the heavens and the earth.") as revealing that the earth, together with the heavens, had been created prior to the Creation sequence of Genesis 1:2b-31. If this interpretation is correct, it may resolve the long-age stellar-light-distance phenomena. .

Expanding on this interpretation, the past tense of Gen 1:1-2a indicates that the heavens were created with the earth, i.e. God had previously created the universe. If the earth "was," then logically, the heavens "were." After verse 2a, the creation process began with the earth as the center of God's creative activity. The light of verse 3 and the 24-hour days that followed came from the earth rotating before the previously created light producing sun. That is, light came on the earth (verse 3) when God removed that which was blocking the sun's light.

To understand Day 4 (Gen 1:14-19) consider this explanation: The word "made" (e.g. "asah" in verse 16) means the use of existing substances for new purposes, in contrast to "create" (e.g. "bara" in verse 1), which word means creating something out of nothing. Concerning Day 4, God "made," that is "established" the existing solar and stellar systems to inform, supply, and regulate life on earth. This interpretation also implies that the creation on this earth recorded in Genesis 1:2b-31 was finished on an "older" earth, which fact may explain various difficult physical dating problems.

However, this particular application of the word "made" (asah) in verse 16 does not appear to satisfy its use in Ex 20:11, "For in six days the Lord made heaven and earth." The verbs "bara" and "asah" are sometimes used interchangeably, and therefore their differences should not be pressed. This second solution has other exegetical problems.

The appendix article, The Stars and Time, addresses the stellar-time issue and seeks to establish that we need not abandon the conviction that this is a young creation.

Chapter 16 Footnotes

1 - The Institute For Creation Research, Impact # 384, June 2005, by Humphreys, D.R. and Morris, J.D., 1996, 149-159, and Ackerman, P.D.

2 - Nature, June 23, 2005, 1067.

3 - Nature, Sept 1, 2005, 46; see Plummer et al, 375.

4 - Technical Journal, Vol 3, 2005, 54.

5 - Two other old-earth theories are Progressive Creation [continuous creation], and the Framework Hypothesis [the first eleven chapters of Genesis are "theological history," not literal history]. These two theories also have serious weaknesses.

6 - Concerning stellar distance measuring methods, see the appendix article, The Stars and Time. Indirect distant measurement methods may be erroneous.

17 - Genealogies

Was the interval of time between the Flood and Abraham long enough for the earth shaking events that began in Peleg's day to materialize? To answer that question we need to analyze significant Biblical genealogies to see the message they convey. We need to see that many Biblical genealogies are not chronologies. We need to demonstrate that the purpose of some of the "father-son" accounts was to establish family lineages and not family chronologies. We need to show that the interval of time between the Flood and Abraham (Genesis 11: 10-27) is not specified.

In Matthew 1:1, we read that Jesus Christ was "the Son of David." Was Jesus Christ the "son" of David? Literally, the answer is "No." Yet we know exactly what Matthew meant by that statement. By saying "Son of", Matthew was saying that Jesus Christ was the "descendant" of David. We know Matthew's meaning because we know the context and know Matthew's purpose: Matthew was affirming that Jesus Christ was fulfilling, legally, the plan of God: Jesus was the Messiah, the promised descendant of David. We see, therefore, that the purpose of Matthew 1:1 also explains Matthew's use of the word "Son." The purpose of Matthew reveals how we should interpret his genealogy. Knowing the purposes of genealogies is necessary to interpret them correctly.

Biblical genealogies use various practices in order to attain desired goals. For example, the author may omit less important names in order to signify a prominent ancestor(s). In addition, the author may use "telescoping" (bringing someone close) to develop a symmetry or parallelism between genealogies. The purposes of some genealogies were legal, for example, inheritance, military service, etc. Other purposes were religious, for example, issues involving Priests and Levites. Other purposes were familial, e.g. establishing bloodlines. Thus, the authors used various literary practices and terminologies to meet specific purposes.

The purposes of Matthew are also demonstrated in the rest of Matthew's genealogy. Matthew concludes his genealogy with this symmetry: "14 and 14 and 14" (verse 17). Matthew has given us a genealogy that we, too, can use and explain, including the beginning and ending of each "14." However, to create that numerical pattern, Matthew left out four men: He left three men out in verse eight and one man in verse eleven. Without an outside source, we would not know that Matthew omitted four men. (See the Supplement below.) That is, we would interpret his wording literally. Furthermore, to create the 14 and 14 and 14 pattern, Matthew had to include a unique relationship: Shealtiel was, apparently, the legal father of Zerubbabel, not his biological father (verse 12). Again, we would not know that precise relationship from the text itself. We would be inclined to interpret that wording literally. These examples illustrate possible meanings of the word "son" and the expressions "fathered" and "father of." Knowing the purpose of a genealogy is important if we are to interpret them correctly. Matthew 1, with its purposes, is an example of a genealogy and not a strict, tight chronology.

The genealogy of Genesis 11 is the family record of the interval between the Flood and Abraham. The thesis of this book is that Genesis 11 is a condensation, that it is a genealogy and not a strict chronology. Consider the following analysis:

1 - The "years" of Genesis 11 are the same as our years. If they were not, but were equivalent to some other unit of time such that the men of Genesis 11 actually lived only 70 of our years, then impossible conditions would result. For example, consider the life of Eber (v16): If his 430 "years" were only 70 of our years, then he became a father when he was only five and one-half years old. If Shem lived only 70 of our years, then Nahor would have lived only 17 years. If the years of Genesis 11 were not our years, many other unreasonable relationships would exist throughout that genealogy. Therefore, the years of Genesis 11 were real years.

2 - If the genealogy of Genesis 11 were a strict chronology, that is, not a condensation whose primary purpose was to give only the lineage from Shem to Abraham, then we have these highly improbable results: The longevities of adjacent generations were unusually reduced. That is, in just nine (apparent) generations, the length of life dropped from 600 years (Shem) to 148 years (Nahor). God's purpose may have been to shorten the length of life of each generation. We cannot rule out that possibility. However, that is a very unlikely explanation. Rather, the large, consecutively reduced longevities indicate that Genesis 11 is a condensation - that generations were omitted from the record.[1] The high probability of the omissions of generations reveals that more years existed in the interval from the Flood to Abraham than a superficial interpretation of the wording of Genesis 11 indicates.

3 - The parallels of the 10 generations of Genesis 11 with the 10 generations of Genesis 5 is comparable with the 14 and 14 and 14 pattern of Matthew 1, which pattern was obtained by the omission of generations.

4 - Genesis 11:26 reveals the flexibility of the expression "fathered." A superficial interpretation of Genesis 11:26 would be that Terah fathered triplets, a suspect interpretation. Though the wording states that Terah fathered Abraham when Terah was 70, we see from Genesis 11:32, 12:4 and Acts 7:4, that Terah was 130 when he fathered Abraham. Therefore, the meaning of verse 26 is that Terah's "fathering" of his three sons *began* when Terah was 70 years old, and that Abraham was born later. We see, therefore, that the word "fathered" has various meanings. The Word is accurate. Our need is to understand it.

5 - If Genesis 11 is not an abridgment, then (1) Noah was a contemporary of Abraham for 50 years; (2) Shem, Shelah, and Eber outlived Abraham; and (3) Eber was a contemporary of Jacob when Jacob worked for Laban. Yet, in the chapters following Genesis 11, no mention is made of these important ancestors. Rather, Joshua describes Abraham's "fathers" as living "of old times beyond the River." (Josh 24:2,14-15)

6 - When we examine, in the Bible, the civilized world that existed at the time of Abraham, we see well-established nations. Those elaborate national, civic and political developments would have been highly unlikely, based on Ussher's [2] tight chronology, i.e. the short 200-year interval since the dispersion from Babel. Nation building needs many years to develop. Moreover, the science of Archeology, even with its secular weaknesses, reveals a greater antiquity for the other civilizations and cultures than 200 years allows.

For a further explanation of these genealogies, see the Supplement below. The most important witness to history is the witness of the Word of God. It must supersede all other witnesses. However, we must be careful not to make the Word say something that the Word is not saying. In conclusion, the Word does not rule out the physical division of Pangaea because the interval from the Flood to Abraham was too short; the Biblical text does not specify the length of that interval.

Chapter 17 Footnotes

1 - For example, based on the example of Matthew 1, an equally valid interpretation of, e.g. Gen 11:16 is the following: "When Eber had lived 34 years, he became the ancestor (or progenitor) of Peleg…."

2 - James Ussher (1581-1656), an Irish Bishop and theologian. He propounded Biblical chronologies. For example, he dated the Creation at 4004 B.C.

Genealogy Supplement

The Genealogy of Matthew 1:

-- Concerning the three men omitted in verse 8 (Ahaziah, Joash, Amaziah), see 2 Chr 21:4– 26:23. See also 2 Kgs 8:25, 11:2, and 14:1.

-- Concerning the man omitted in verse 11 (Jehoiakim), see 2 Chr 36:1-9. See also 2 Kgs 23:34 and 1 Chr 3:16

-- Concerning Shealtiel's relation to Zerubbabel, see 1 Chr 3:17-19. See also Ezr 3:2,8; Neh 12:1; and Hg 1:12,14 and 2:2,23.

Flexibility and liberal use of the word "son":

-- Obed, the son of Ruth, is called the "son" of Naomi (Ru 4:17)

-- Compare Ezr 7:1-5 with 1 Chr 6:3-14. Ezra omits six men after Meraioth. Moreover, Ezr 8:1-2 is an abridgment, because these "sons" were not literally sons but descendants.

Genealogies involving Moses:

-- Levi, Judah, and Joseph were brothers together in Egypt. Their contemporary descendents were, respectively, Moses, Bezaleel, and Joshua. Moses' genealogy records only two men between Levi and Moses. Five men are recorded between Judah and Bezaleel. However, *nine* men are recorded between Joseph and Joshua. Moreover, the same 430 year period is required to bridge the time between the three brothers and these contemporary descendents. While Joshua's genealogy appears to be complete, men must have been omitted in the genealogy before Moses and in the genealogy before Bezaleel. For example, if Moses' genealogy was not abridged, then Moses' "grandfather," Kohath, had 17,200 grandchildren! (Nm 3:17-19, 27-28).

-- (For the "430" years, see Ex 12:40. However, a question exists: when did the 430 period begin? For the genealogies see Gen 41:50-52; Ex 17:10, 31:1-6, and 35:22-26; 1 Chr 6:1-3, 2:3-5, 18-20 and 7:20-27.)

-- From 1 Chr 26:24 we see that Shebuel was not the immediate son, but a distant son of Gershom who was the actual son of Moses (Ex 2:21-22).

Conclusion: Many Scriptures indicate that Genesis 11 is not a strict chronology.

18 – Conclusion

The Genesis Flood destroyed the surface of the earth. The Flood formed fossil-filled, earth covering strata. Inertial forces gradually generated energies that deformed the horizontal strata-covered crust, formed the mountains, and divided the one land, Pangaea, into continents. Those forces, stresses, and energies were produced by the "permanently misplaced" waters, the amazingly lowered ocean, and the immense revolving north and south glaciers. The separated continents further divided peoples and distributed animals.

This brief summary is consistent with the Genesis Record. Moreover, that physical history strongly indicates that stresses and earthquakes will increase as our remnant glaciers melt.

Almost all of Genesis is a clear account of early history. Yet, a few aspects of that record are enigmatic. One uncertain subject is the "division" of Peleg. Because of a lack of geologic and genealogical knowledge, a common conviction is that Peleg's division was social or political or familial, but not physical. This book seeks to prove that Peleg's Division was physical, and the division occurred within a young earth period. The supporting evidence includes many geologic phenomena, the fossil bearing and deformed strata, the glacial debris, the harmonious matching of the continents, etc. The geologic evidence beautifully supports the Genesis record of the Flood and Peleg's Division. This book also seeks to establish that essentially all physical and anthropological evidence supports a young world. The evidence is that Peleg's Division occurred recently, and the ages required by the theory of Evolution simply did not exist.

Asserting that continental separations never occurred damages the witness of the Word. The world knows that the continents have separated. Faithful to the Word, we need to explain Peleg's Division to those willing to listen. This explanation is far superior to secular theories concerning "continental drift." For example, the phenomena of deformed strata testify to the recent forces of Peleg's Day; the ubiquitous bent strata contradict long-age theories. Explaining the why and how of Peleg's Division is necessary if we are to advance the Truth, remove barriers to the Faith, and weaken the world's justification for dismissing Biblical history. Declaring the truth will bear good fruit

Affirming the division of Pangaea is more significant than removing a witnessing weakness. Affirming Peleg's physical division helps establish a sound and significant worldview. Peleg's Division affected many peoples, cultures, and histories. Like the Flood, that great division profoundly affected the physical world. Peleg's Division is a critical part of historical geology. Peleg's Division is necessary for understanding both earth history and human history.

We need to integrate Peleg into world history. One benefit will be its cleansing effect concerning the evil of Evolution. More important, affirming Peleg's Division helps establish the veracity and value of Biblical history.

APPENDIX

The Second Law of Thermodynamics

The 2nd Law has many expressions, many applications. The Law states that in an isolated system, that is, in a system without an energy input and an ordering input, the isolated system naturally goes from order to disorder, from high energy to low energy, from complexity to simplicity, from high information to low information, etc. Isolated systems do not naturally go the other way. That means isolated systems need outside "help" to go from disorder to order, from low information to high information, etc. Because nothing is outside of it, the universe is an isolated system to which the 2nd Law applies.[1] Furthermore, the earth is, essentially, a "closed" system. Though the earth has an energy input, that is, the sun, it does not have an external ordering input. Therefore, living systems on earth become less complex with time, not more. They do not "evolve." That is exactly what we observe. For example, mutations are almost always, if not always, genetically disordering and produce a loss of complexity and information. Therefore, the over all trend for living systems is downward, not upward.

Evolution claims that "pockets" of increasing complexity temporarily exist by virtue of appropriating the loss of complexity and energy elsewhere, and therefore evolution may occur in these pockets. However, this claim does not negate the universal embrace of the 2nd Law.

Concerning the beginning of the 2nd Law, it did not begin with the Curse. The 2nd Law was and is a natural part of the Creation, because the 2nd Law is an integral part of the natural functions of the science of physics. However, with the Curse, God removed from nature His ordering power that countered the disordering aspects inherent in the 2nd Law. With the Curse, God enabled the 2nd Law to have its full power to disorder. (How God applied His ordering power to the original Creation to keep it harmonious and beautiful and then, with the Curse, removed this ordering power, is unknown.) His removal is manifest in God taking from Adam and Eve the potential He had given them for eternal life. For example, the biological repair mechanisms God built into their cells and bodies (and ours) would no longer be completely adequate to keep them from death. However, immediately with the Curse, in His prepared plan of love and grace, God promised the Gospel (Genesis 3:15), that is, the redeeming work of the Messiah and His final removal of the Curse.

In an effort to support the Theory of Evolution, some evolutionists try, in vain, to explain away the truth of the 2nd Law. For example, in the book, <u>Into the Cool: Energy Flow, Thermodynamics and Life,</u> two evolutionists try to explain how order develops out of disorder. Reviewing their book, another evolutionist said plainly, "…the authors' claim…falls flat!" [2]

Complexity is an aspect of order. Extreme complexity in cells, body systems, etc. is obvious evidence of the ordering input of Intelligence. Furthermore, our physical Laws are so very fine-tuned that not only can biological life exist, but also our physical universe. Life and the universe would not exist if the physical constants of nature were changed even slightly. All these evidences verify the input of the Intelligent Designer, our wonderful God. With these many evidences, it is foolish for the logical person not to believe.

Yet, these conditions prevail: "For what can be known about God is plain to them, because God has shown it to them….in the things that have been made….but they became futile in their thinking….they became fools." (Romans 1:19-22) Concerning those who do not believe, the problem is not the evidence, but the heart. They will not believe in the origin and effects of the Curse, but use the reality of evil, social disorder, disease, and death to justify their unbelief in the witness of our miraculous creation and of our loving God.

2ⁿᵈ Law Footnote:
1 - See the appendix article, The Stars and Time.
2 - Nature, August 4, 2005, 627.

The Earth

The three basic parts of the earth are its core, mantle, and crust. See figure 14. The radius of the earth is about 3980 miles. The radius of the core is about 2180 miles. The thickness of the mantle is about 1800 miles. However, the mantle contains 84 percent while the core only 15 percent of the earth's volume. (Together they constitute slightly more than 99% of the earth's mass.) The core appears to consist mostly of iron. It is very hot. The mantle, also hot, consists primarily of silicates (the bonding of oxygen and silicon) in combination with other metallic atoms. The density of the earth as a whole is two times as dense as its crust.

The crust is rigid, even brittle. The crust is of two types: oceanic and continental. Oceanic crust averages three to four miles thick. Continental crust varies more in thickness. Because the continents are floating on the mantle, the continental crust is thickest under mountain ranges, e.g. 30 miles thick, because the weight of the mountains on the mantle is greatest there. Both crusts consist primarily of silicates combined with other atoms. Oceanic crust, a fine-grained (small crystals) igneous rock, is usually termed "basaltic." Continental crust, usually a coarse-grained (large crystals) igneous rock, is called "granitic." Oceanic crust is heavier than continental crust, because its silicates are combined with heavier atoms. The bottom of both crusts is called the "Moho," (named after Andrija Mohorovicic, who identified it). The Moho, too, is rigid. The topmost layer of the mantle is also rigid. These three top layers of the earth are called the "lithosphere." The differences between these three layers appear to be chemical and not mechanical. That is, these three layers appear to be mechanically bonded and work together as a unit in determining the earth's plates.

As we have stated, the lithosphere is about as thin to the earth as the shell of a hard boiled egg is to the egg. It is very thin relative to the whole earth. The lithosphere occupies slightly more than 1 percent of the earth's volume but about 1 percent of its mass. Realizing how thin the lithosphere is helps put into perspective the reasonable probabilities of crustal deformations and Pangaea's division.

The layer below the lithosphere is the portion of the mantle that controls, that is, inhibits or permits and facilitates the movements of the earth's plates. It is the so-called "weak" layer. The difference between this mantle layer and the mantle layer above it appears to be mechanical and not chemical, although water in the weak layer may be a factor.[1] This layer is called the "asthenosphere" ("asthenos" means "weak" in Greek.). The evidence is accumulating that most magmas (liquid rock) that penetrate the lithosphere and erupts onto the surface of the earth originate in this layer.

The asthenosphere played a critical part in the division of Pangaea. The asthenosphere worked as a barrier between the lithosphere, which is rigid, and the mantle below the asthenosphere. Because of the isolating effect of the asthenosphere, (stresses were not readily transmitted through it) much of the potential energies – except heat energy – were stored in the lithosphere. Pangaea's division finally resulted from the ever-increasing energies in the lithosphere.

Crust vs. Lithosphere: This book uses the expression "crust" in a general sense. Because the crust is the top layer of the lithosphere, it is convenient to let the crust represent the lithosphere. This is the practice of this book, because it is the crust that receives the external forces. Furthermore, this is also the terminology practice in scientific literature.

Seismic Waves: The earth's construction and other characteristics are determined by analyzing the earth's vibrations. Earthquakes are the usual source for these vibrations. These vibrations have different characteristics: "P" waves, which compress and stretch rock, and "S" waves, which shake rock from side to side. The earth responds differently to these vibrations, such as the velocities and the penetrations of the vibrations through the various regions of the earth. In particular, P waves penetrate all types of rocks, including the molten and liquid types. P waves, which travel faster, are usually less destructive. S waves cannot penetrate molten and liquid rock. However, though slower then P waves, S waves are usually more destructive. Analyzing the responses to these vibrations, geologists can, probably, determine distances, densities, pressures, temperatures, some chemical characteristics, plasticity and liquidity.

The New Geology: The phenomena of Plate Tectonics have opened new doors for the science of geology. Plate Tectonics has helped in understanding the earth's geology and actions, especially the practical problem of earthquakes. However, as we have stated, geologic science is not fully finding the truth, because it rejects the clear input from the Word.

The Earth Footnote:

1 - "A sharp lithosphere-asthenosphere boundary….": Nature, July 28, 2005, 542

The Stars and Time

The purpose of this article is to provide insight concerning the age of the universe. First, we will review some fundamentals. Then we will analyze the popular secular theory about the origin, size and age of the universe. Lastly, we will apply the fundamentals to that modern stellar theory and to problems relevant to the age issue.

Time is the primary subject of this article. God, our wonderful Father, is the Lord of time. He has given us, His children, created in His image, the ability to analyze time, to think complex thoughts about time. However, unlike God, we are bound by time. To define our "time" subject accurately, we must differentiate it from our imprecise ways of thinking about time. The subject of this article is not "mental time," but "physical time," the time-laws controlling all physical processes. Physical time embraces all changes, all rates and dynamic phenomena, from the atomic to the stellar. Laws control this time precisely. We, created in the image of God, can stand apart and analyze these time-laws. This article examines the characteristics of physical time and its stellar manifestations.

We begin with a review of fundamentals. The environment in which time is transpiring determines the dimensions of physical time. (Environment-independent time measuring clocks do not exist!) For example, consider time's laws in the propagation of light energy, the photon. With respect to the entire universe, the velocity of light in the universe is apparently constant. Furthermore, regardless of how fast we move in the universe, or our directions, the velocity of the light we measure is always the same. This is amazing! For light velocities to be always the same, as we measure them, the dimensions of time and distance in our local, moving, environment must correspondingly change to produce those constant light velocities. That is, with motion, time slows and distances decrease correspondingly. Thus, the dimensions of time are relative and change according to the velocity of our environment. Physical time is flexible; it is relative.

In addition, gravity affects physical time, the phenomenon measured by a clock. (This is reasonable, because gravity is a manifestation of acceleration, the derivative of velocity.) A clock runs faster (38.4 microseconds per day) in a global position system (GPS) satellite, where gravity on that GPS clock is weaker, than the same clock on the surface of the earth where gravity is stronger. Thus, all atomic and chemical rates (including the aging of our bodies) and all other rates increase as the surrounding gravitational strengths are reduced. Therefore, we must include the phenomena of the gravitational acceleration ("inflation") of time when determining the ages that stellar distances seem to indicate.

Again, concerning light, from what we have discussed concerning the gravitational effects on time in physical processes, it should not surprise us that gravity also affects light. The photon, with its inherent time component (its frequency), reacts to gravitational fields. For instance, the strong gravitational field of the sun bends starlight.

Furthermore, gravitational fields draw energy from photons. Consider the following: The energy of a photon is directly proportional to its frequency. For example, the frequency of violet light is almost twice the frequency of red light, and therefore violet light is almost twice as energetic as red light. (Ultraviolet light, with a still higher frequency, is damaging!) Therefore, gravity's effect on the color of light is indicative. That is, as the gravitational field draws energy from the photon passing through the field, the photon's frequency must be reduced. Thus, passing through a gravitational field, violet light, losing energy, is transformed *toward* red light. Gravity reddens light.[1]

Continually moving the source of light away from the observer also reduces the frequency of light toward the red. This is the "Doppler effect." Moving the light source away stretches the emitted photon's wavelength and therefore lowers its frequency. However, light transformed toward the red may be caused by gravity fields and not necessarily by stellar motion. We will apply these facts in our analysis.

The last fundamental in this review is the "geography" of the universe. Is the universe the same in every direction everywhere or does it have a boundary? Clearly, if the universe is the same in every direction everywhere then it does not have a center, a "privileged point." Conversely, if the universe has a privileged point, a center, then it is not the same in every direction everywhere and is bounded. This significant distinction affects the results of cosmology.

These velocity, acceleration, gravity, time, light and spatial fundamentals are important in analyzing stellar phenomena.

Now we consider theories of the universe: Secular theories try to explain, without our creator God, the origin and processes of the starry universe. Amazingly, their "scientific" theories are filled with explanations that contradict sound scientific fundamentals. The prevailing secular theories of the universe can be put under the umbrella popularly called "Big Bang Cosmology" (BBC). According to BBC, about 13.7 billion years ago, a tiny kernel of extreme energy, in much less than a billionth of a second, suddenly expanded. Its instantaneous expansion created space, billions of light-years across, and time, physical time. As the big bang's energy expanded and therefore its temperature dropped, subatomic particles developed. As the temperature continued to drop, these particles combined to form simple atoms, e.g. hydrogen. These atoms, drawn together by gravity, contracted to produce hydrogen nuclear reactions, that is, stars. Those so-called first generation stars consisted of just the simpler atoms. Then aging, some of those stars exploded producing supernovas, which explosions produced pressures sufficient to force the simpler atoms together to produce heavier, more complex atoms. This star creating and exploding process, repeated many times, continued throughout billions of years to produce all the complex 92 elements. Somehow, this stellar building process formed millions of galaxies of millions and billions of stars each. Finally, 4.6 billion years ago, our sun, a "third generation" star, and our sun's solar system of the planets and our earth, began to be formed. This is a brief story of BBC.

What are the scientific problems with BBC theory? They are many! Here are a few: Before the big bang, what was the history (?) of that tiny energy ball that burst? (Before BBC - a "before" BBC did not exist!) How did it get to possess such an unbelievable high level of energy? How did the ball get the capacity to produce complex atomic and stellar order? BBC theories have no reasonable scientific answers!

No matter how far back its "history" (?) is taken, that tiny energy ball had to obey the 1st Law of Thermodynamics, that is that energy and matter cannot be created. Yet that tiny ball broke the 1st Law because it had no explainable source for its energy. That tiny ball also broke the 2nd Law, because isolated systems only go toward disorder. How did that tiny ball produce highly ordered subatomic particles and then atoms, stars and galaxies. Again, no prior, external ordering source existed to produce all that order.

Expanding on what we have outlined, BBC theory asks us to believe that the very high energy released - by some laws, some "orders" from somewhere - became partial subatomic particles, which particles organized themselves to produce atomic particles like protons, neutrons and electrons, which particles then organized themselves to produce hydrogen atoms. Gravitational attraction - somehow gravity was produced - then drew the hydrogen atoms together, which when concentrated, produced temperatures that fused the hydrogen atoms to form helium atoms (and probably other simple atoms) with the release of great energy, i.e. nuclear reactions. Thus, stars developed.

(Supposedly, a half billion to a billion years were needed to reach the star-stage. However, according to sound physical principles, gasses do not, of themselves with the pull of gravity, condense and fuse. As gases contract and compact, temperature increases create backpressures, which pressures inhibit continued gas contraction. Secular theory recognizes this problem: The theory knows that to form stars, external pressures were required to concentrate the gases. However, in the initial stages of BBC, no stars existed to explode, so no external pressures around those gases would ever be produced. Star formation never "got off the ground"!)

Let us assume stars were somehow produced. We continue the BBC story: Some of the stars then broke down, exploded, and thereby with new radiant pressures, fused the hydrogen, helium and other simple atoms to produce more complex atoms. The star-evolving and star-exploding sequences continued for billions of years and, with internal heat, fused existing atoms into ever heavier and more complex atoms until, finally, all the various 92 natural elements that we now have were produced. This description of the development of the stars and of all the elements omits many details. However, it outlines BBC theory enough to present this highly improbable atomic development, the origin of matter – all on its own.

Continuing the fact of the breaking of the 2nd Law of Thermodynamics are the phenomena of the development of the countless elaborate galaxies, each with billions of stars. These include our own Milky Way galaxy, and our solar system, all producing order out of disorder. The BBC story, this breaking of the 2nd Law, the unnatural movement from simplicity to complexity, is explained by claiming that, "before" BBC (?), i.e. *inherent* in that tiny energy ball were the capabilities needed to govern the sequences that generated all the complexities of the 92 elements, and also the many majestic stellar formations – without outside help. These claims are incredulous! But, if secular scientists must leave God out, they must come up with theories, even if the theories are contrary to fundamental laws, explanations hard to accept.

Supposedly, BBC produced many other physical "Laws" which were so exquisitely and finely tuned that, collectively, they are called the "Anthropic Cosmological Principle." (Anthropic is from the Greek word for man, "anthropos.") These laws enabled not only this physical universe to exist, but also all forms of life. That BBC should have produced these fortuitous, finely balanced laws and relationships from the big bang, and by accident – which secular theory maintains it did - is very difficult to believe.

What is the evidence used to support such an incredible BBC story? The phenomena are primarily two: the red shift of stellar light, and background radiation. The red shift phenomena supposedly prove that the big bang occurred 13.7 billion years ago, and that the universe is still expanding. The background radiation is supposedly the residual energy from the great energy release of the big bang. Consider the evidence:

Red shift: A star gives off light. If the star is moving away from the viewer, because of light's fixed velocity, the wavelength of its radiation is stretched making it longer and therefore its frequency lower, and therefore all the light frequencies from the star are shifted toward the red end of the light spectrum. The faster the star is moving away, the more the wavelength is stretched and therefore the redder the light becomes. The light from the "nearer" stars, not moving away as fast, is shifted only slightly toward the red. The light from the stars supposedly further away and moving faster, is shifted more, and the reddest stars are the fastest and furthest. These red shifts supposedly indicate the universe's expansion. With backward extrapolation, these red shifts supposedly prove that a big bang occurred 13.7 billion years ago. This burst created expanding space and thus moved the (to-be-formed) stars apart with the reddest stars at the leading edge of the expansion. BBC maintains that the motion of the stars is primarily from the expansion *of* space, not the movement of stars *into* preexisting space. BBC *made* space!

Background radiation: Because the big bang occurred so long ago, all that remains of its energy is a very low-level radiation. (Low-level radiation is measurable.) Supposedly, this radiation is proof that the big bang did occur.

Now we need to apply our initial fundamentals to the issues of time. First, a word about stellar distances: Though the angles are very small, triangulation can determine the distances to local stars up to a distance of about 300 light-years. For stars beyond triangulation, indirect means, such as light intensities, are used. Finally, based on the secular theory of an expanding universe and the movements of the stars in that expanding space, BBC theory is applied using the principle that the star's distance is proportional to its degree of redness. Built on these criteria, the farthest stars are, supposedly, over ten billion light years away.

(Only galaxies, not individual stars, can be seen at great distances. Reservations exist about the veracity of these distances: the hierarchy of indirect measurement methods, with theories built on theories, are suspect; the extreme stellar distances accepted today may not be valid.)

(Rigorous mathematics and physics are required to analyze, adequately, complex stellar phenomena.[2] The following analyses of BBC and distance-time phenomena are only brief, limited, and suggested solutions to the time issue.)

Concerning the evidence of the background radiation, this is a weak proof for BBC. With the millions and billions of stars and galaxies in the universe, it would be surprising if "background" radiation did not exist. These stars and galaxies are like hot furnaces emitting many radiations. Too many unknowns exist to claim that the low-level radiation now measured is the background radiation from the supposed big bang.

The second evidence claimed to prove the big bang, stellar red shift, is more significant. We begin with the issue of the "geography" of the universe. BBC maintains that the universe has no privileged point. That is, no place in the universe is more central than any other place. However, that BBC theory is purely arbitrary – it has no proof. BBC advocates that principle because BBC theorists do not want to repeat the type of error that Copernicus (16th century) had to correct, i.e. the error that the earth was at the center, and the sun, planets, and stars rotated around the earth. BBC arbitrarily maintains that the universe has no center.

However, the universe may indeed have a center, and the earth may be at or near that center. (The "earth" in this analysis represents our solar system, which system is an extremely small part of the universe.) Red shifts exist in every direction from the earth, a possible indication of the earth's centrality. Furthermore, stars and galaxies are not the same in every direction from the earth. Contrary to BBC, asymmetries exist. Moreover, the Word implies our centrality: the Creator of the universe created and then came to this earth! The contrast between these two geographies produces very different results.

Assuming the apparent and probable centrality of the earth, red shifts may be explained in several ways. First, the universe around the earth may be expanding, and the red shift phenomena are a fact; for good reasons, God may have created the universe to be in an expansion mode. ("God made the expanse...."Gen 1:7) If so, red shifts do not indicate billions of years of time. Second, as we have seen, physical time rates are subject to velocity, acceleration, and gravity. With a non-expanding universe, the rates of time-change in regions far from the earth, as we perceive them, may be far faster than our own local rates. God's "expanse" probably created vast and contrasting physical time scales. Therefore, time-controlled physical indicators may not dictate time dimensions that negate a young universe. Third, gravity reddens light. With a non-expanding universe, and with the distances light travels through gravity fields from the outer regions of the universe, gravity gradients may cause the red shifts that we see. Therefore, red shifts may not be due to stellar motion. Red shifts may be a "tired light" phenomena. Moreover, *a star's emitted light may be red-shifted.*[3] In conclusion, red shifts are not an unquestionable proof of "millions of earth years."

The universe is breathtaking. The more we see the more awesome it becomes. Mysteries fill the universe. This brief analysis, with its limitations, has surely not explained all the phenomena. However, concerning time, we should not bow the knee to secular science and revere its *very* questionable claims, while we question and put God and His Word in second place.

The Stars and Time footnotes:

1 - Our eyes do not perceive this change. In this frequency shift, invisible ultraviolet moves to [become] visible violet, violet to blue, blue to green, green to yellow, and yellow to red. Therefore, we see no change. Only instruments can detect reddening shifts.

Some physicists doubt that gravity absorbs photon energy and reddens light.

2 - The following books should be considered:

Faulkner, D., Universe By Design, Master Books, Green Forest, AR, © 2004

Humphreys, D.R., Starlight and Time, Master Books, Colorado Springs, CO, © 1994

Mulfinger, G. Jr., Ed., Design and Origins in Astronomy, CRS Books, © 1983

Williams, A., & Hartnett, J., Dismantling the Big Bang, Green Forest, AR, © 2005

3 - A. Einstein: "An atom...emits light of a frequency dependent on...the gravitational field in which it is situated." (Relativity: The Special and General Theory, 1952, p130.)

Historical Conflict and Geologic Evidence

The following article from a 1967 issue of Time magazine (8/18/67) is illuminating. It shows the conflict that existed between the old school of geologic thought and the new school concerning continental drift, and some of the geologic evidence that helped change the old school's thinking:

TIME Magazine

Piecing Continents Together Were all continents once snuggled together in a mammoth land mass...? Some scientists believe so, and many recent findings support them. This month still more compelling evidence of continental drift was reported by U.S. and Brazilian geologists. Their principal finding was that two highly distinctive adjacent geological areas of the Atlantic coast of Africa match perfectly with a pair of rock regions located along Brazil's northeast coast.

Doubting & Digging "Actually, we set out to disprove the theory when we started," said M.I.T. Geology Professor Patrick M. Hurley, 55, adding that "Harvard and M.I.T. have been hotbeds of geological conservatism for years." Hurley and his colleagues became interested in the theory at a 1964 scientific meeting in London. There, Cambridge Geophysicist Sir Edward Bullard disclosed that a computer study of shorelines on both sides of the Atlantic – at a depth of 500 fathoms [3000 feet], to allow for coastal idiosyncrasies – showed that they would still match if they were set side by side. "The results were rather amazing," said Hurley. "The study went right down the whole Atlantic and fitted together everything, including Greenland and all the other islands with less than one degree error in the fit."

Still leery of the theory, Hurley returned to the U.S. and organized a joint group of U.S. and Brazilian scientists to compare...rock samples from two African regions with others from South American areas. The African regions are divided neatly by a boundary running northeast through Ghana....According to Bullard, if the South American bulge had once fitted under the bulge of Africa, the continuance of the delineation between the two rock regions would be found running southwest through Brazil from a point near the city of Sao Luis....

[Hurley said] "when I began to plot these (rock) samples, the correlation was astounding. They all fit together exactly." In addition...Hurley, his M.I.T. associates and their collaborators at the University of Sao Paulo, found the boundary line...exactly where they had predicted it would be.

The discovery provides important support for the continental-drift theory...."To us, this evidence is quite conclusive," says Hurley. "It's very difficult to argue against it. It looks as though opposition to the continental-drift theory is dying."

Folk Lore and History

The Flood of Genesis profoundly affected the history of all races and peoples. All came from the sons of Noah. It is therefore not surprising that essentially all races and peoples have in their traditions stories about the Flood. It is also not surprising that after thousands of years, their various Flood stories differ. However, enough similarities exist that we can see in their stories the outline of the Flood event. These cultural phenomena of Flood traditions are an excellent witness to the reality of the Flood.

The division of Pangaea was another world-encompassing event. It was an event witnessed by men. Moreover, God, in His wisdom, recorded that event in the Bible. However, Pangaea's division, though global, contrasts with the Flood. Apparently, Pangaea's division did not significantly affect everyone. Many people groups, in the center of landmasses, probably knew nothing, first hand, of the divisions that took place. It had not materially affected them. Though in time they probably received word, this global event did little to influence their folk lore.

On the other hand, Pangaea's division must have profoundly affected some people groups. A separation may have gone right through the center of their country, a devastating phenomenon. Or a division may have separated them from a neighboring people with whom they traded, or made war. The division may have been so significant that that event took a permanent place in their folk lore. Indeed, that appears to be the case. Considerable folk lore exists concerning lost lands and lost civilizations. The Lost Civilization of Atlantis is a familiar example.[1] Moreover, lost lands and civilizations received much attention and acceptance in recent centuries.

Today, archeological and anthropological discoveries in eastern North America, Central and South America are finding the evidences of settlements and developed civilizations whose antiquities are so remote that the previous standard explanations for getting those people there, in time, no longer suffice. With the Glacial Epoch dominating Canada, migrating from Asia through Alaska would be very difficult if not impossible. The explanation that these peoples came by way of the Bering Land Bridge is becoming increasingly unacceptable. "Who the earliest Americans were and how they got there is one of anthropology's biggest riddles."[2] The time needed to develop those American civilizations requires another explanation.[3]

Given the archeological, historical and geological facts, the evidence is excellent that the settlements and civilizations of the Americas were already there *before* Pangaea divided. The probabilities are very good that, due to the division of Pangaea, the histories of these people, their civilizations, and others elsewhere, provided the historical basis for some lost-land folk lore.[4]

Folk Lore and History Footnotes

1 - Concerning Atlantis, the Greek philosopher, Plato, recounting folk lore he had received, said the following: "There occurred violent earthquakes and floods...and in a single day...the island...disappeared in the depths of the sea." Plato said that an advanced civilization and powerful kingdom inhabited a very large island that was located off the coast of Northwestern Africa. Science/ScienceNow (on-line), "Atlantis Rises Again,"

Genevra Ornelas, July 22, 2005, and the <u>Encyclopedia Britannica</u> article, "Atlantis."

2 - Science, July 25, 2003, 450.

3 - We need to recognize the dating weaknesses of secular archeology. With these reservations in mind, the following are some archeological finds: The secular standard in archeology for the earliest Americans has been, for years, the "Clovis" people of New Mexico, dated approximately 11,500 years ago. (Archeologists differ on this Clovis dating. Supposedly, Clovis came via Alaska, though hard evidence of such a migration is lacking. Furthermore, archeologists differ on this migration theory also.) Contradictions exist to this standard theory: older human remains have been found in Chile. Furthermore, their artifacts are like those of Europeans who lived in southern France and Spain, indicating that the Chileans came from Europe. ("Were Spaniards Among the First Americans." Science, Nov 19, 1999, 1467.) Human remains and drawings have been found in caves near the mouth of the Amazon River in Brazil with approximately the same Clovis dating. (Science, April 19, 1995, 346, 373.) Human remains and artifacts in Eastern North America have been dated to 14,000 years ago. (The Washington Post Magazine, April 1, 2001, 28; Science, July 30, 2004, 590.) Some human remains in South America have, supposedly, been dated to over 20,000 years. (Scientific American, September 2000, 80.) Furthermore, the skull characteristics of the Clovis people – short and wide skulls with relatively flat faces – are different from the other American skulls. (Science, Dec 23, 2005, 1900.) All this evidence indicates that the different peoples in the Americas came from separate lands, and not via Alaska. Whence were these lands?

4 - A lost-land more significant than Atlantis, particularly in recent centuries, is the lost land called "Lemuria." Lemuria was believed to be located south of India and toward Madagascar, though there are other traditions concerning its location. (Many of the Tamil people of South India and Sri Lanka consider Lemuria as the land in which their culture, language, and history began.) During the 17th, 18th, and 19th centuries, many European scientists and historians seriously believed that Lemuria was historical. These Europeans produced a considerable literature with subjects such as the probability that Lemuria was a land bridge for the distribution of plants and animals within the southern hemisphere. However, as uniformitarianism displaced catastrophism in western thinking, and then as the theory of continental drift developed, serious consideration that Lemuria was historical have almost disappeared.

The mysteries of lost lands have provided an environment for occultism, new-age ideologies and false religions. These distressing developments have created a fog and bias that has hampered historical research concerning lost lands.

For more information about Lemuria, see Ramaswamy.

Problems

The division and separation of Pangaea provides reasonable explanations to problems that have been difficult to answer:

(1) How did many identical, dissimilar, and unique forms of life get to lands now widely separated by seas? For example, Australia has unique animals.

Answer: After the Flood, but before Peleg, with all lands connected, these life forms migrated to those lands, or were carried there. After Peleg, with continental separation, these life forms became isolated. This explanation applies to people groups also. Furthermore, even following the division of Pangaea, while the glaciers were melting and sea levels were still low, land bridges probably continued for many years and only disappeared after most of the glaciers had melted. For further discussion, see the appendix article, Folk Lore and History.

(2) From the secular worldview, why do the Atlantic Ocean basins have far less sediments than they should have?

Answer: The development of the Atlantic basins occurred recently, only following continental separation. These ocean basins are young.

(3) From the secular worldview, why do the eastern basins of the Pacific Ocean have far less sediments than they should have?

Answer: The Pacific was part of Pangaea's original ocean. With the separation of the Americas, their western movements subducted the eastern sediments that were on the Pacific plates.

(4) If the original land of the Creation was divided, why do we still have the Tigris and Euphrates Rivers of Genesis 2:14?

Answer: This question is irrelevant to the issue of the division of Pangaea and the thesis of this book. However, because this question may be asked, the following is the answer to that question: In America, we have a "Cambridge," a "London," a "Berlin," a "Rome," and a "Moscow." In other words, the people of the New World carried over names from the Old World. Actually, the Flood destroyed and obliterated the surface of Pangaea, including those original two rivers. The phenomenon of naming post-Flood rivers came from names carried over from the pre-Flood world.

These naming phenomena existed in Biblical times: Cuneiform tablets reveal that Babylonian exiles, including the Jews, were located in their own communities, and there they gave their new towns the same names as the towns from which they came. See the article by Andre Lemaire, 57-59, 67 in Biblical Archeology Review, Nov – Dec, 2005.

(5) Does not the existence of Mt. Ararat of Genesis 8:4 contradict the assertion that almost all mountain building came during the years of Pangaea's division, a time that was much later than the Flood.

Answer: God made a pleasant place for Adam and Eve. Knowing their nature and what would be pleasing to them - we like variety - God probably made granitic mountains for them to enjoy. Therefore, some mountains must have existed before the Flood.

Problems

The sedimentary rock record verifies the Scriptures that the pre-Flood world was devastated. The eroding power of those moving waters is almost beyond our comprehension. We do not know how many of those original mountains survived the Flood. However, some probably survived. Concerning the original creation, volcanoes did not exist: they are very destructive, both locally and globally. As we have discussed under the subject, "Earthquakes," volcanoes began during the Flood and have continued since. Mt. Ararat in Eastern Turkey was a volcanic mountain. The eruptions of hot lava built its structure. Therefore, it is questionable that the Mt. Ararat of today is the same Mount Ararat of Genesis 8:4. (This identity of names should not surprise us. Refer to question four above.) The Ark may have landed on a granitic mountain that survived the Flood. That mountain was probably located somewhere in the Middle East. Traditions exist that the Ark landed on the Zagros Mountains of Western Iran, mountains just east of Babylon. The Zagros Mountains contain sedimentary rocks, which also raises questions about the reliability of those traditions. However, those mountains, as well as Mount Ararat in Eastern Turkey may have had some pre Flood granitic cores. Questions about the location of Biblical Mt. Ararat exist.

Further Research

Paleomagnetism

One argument that the separation of Pangaea took millions of years is based on the evidence of the residual magnetism found symmetrically imprinted in the basalts on each side of the Mid Atlantic Ridge. This argument assumes (1) it takes thousands of years for the earth's magnetic field to change direction, and (2) the basalts were produced by the symmetrical, long term spreading magmas originating in the Ridge, and (3) as the continents moved apart, these spreading magmas captured the earth's changing magnetic fields as the magmas were hardening. Therefore, to estimate the Atlantic Ocean's spreading time, count the number of captured magnetic reversals (paleomagnetism) and then add together the supposed time interval between each reversal.

Assuming the correctness of the interpretation of this geologic data, this is an effective argument for the very slow division of Pangaea. However, there may be reasonable short-term alternatives. Consider the following proposal: The movement of an electric charge produces a magnetic field. Therefore, while Pangaea was rapidly dividing, if electric currents that alternately changed directions passed through the upper mantle, the same "paleomagnetism" results would have been produced. Conducting charges (ions) undoubtedly existed in the hot, liquid magmas and the waters that together were lubricating the movements of the separating landmasses. The movements of the landmasses, in turn, would produce movements of those electric charges, which then would produce magnetic fields.[1] Large and changing current patterns may have developed in the process. These patterns could have produced the paleomagnetic imprints in the spreading basalts – all in a relatively short period.

This theory is a proposal. The phenomena of paleomagnetism need further research. However, an argument against the secular paleomagnetic claim is this question: What valid evidence exists that the earth's central – not local - magnetic field reverses?

Antarctica and Greenland Ice Cores

A second area needing further research concerns the ice cores taken from deep within the glaciers of Antarctica and Greenland. Falling snow should capture and enclose many of the characteristics of the atmosphere through which the snow passed. Hopefully, the compacted snow that turned into glacial ice created an accurate record of those atmospheric conditions. The ice cores should then reveal these conditions. These are some of the characteristics probably recorded in the ice cores: atmospheric dust, air temperature, precipitation, volcanic sulfates, oxygen isotope ratios,[2] carbon dioxide and other gases. Ice cores are analyzed to determine past conditions such as atmospheric temperatures, an area of study for those concerned with global warming.

However, our concern is dating – how old are the glaciers. Secular dating from these cores supposedly proves that these glaciers gradually formed over hundreds of thousands of years. However, the results of those tests and the conclusions reached depend almost entirely on the world-view assumptions that were the basis of those analyses. That is, if the secular Pleistocene time-frame is assumed in the analyses, the data will be interpreted to support that time-frame. A good example of biased analysis is the uniformitarian, long-age interpretation of the sedimentary rock record. But that interpretation of the rock record has proven to be very inadequate and erroneous. (In the mid 20th century, secular geology introduced neocatastrophism – a partial corrective.) Secular ice core dating, based on uniformitarian assumptions, will probably prove to be equally erroneous.

A fundamental assumption of secular ice core analysis is uniformitarianism. Their philosophy assumes essentially uniform rates of snowfall over thousands of years. But that assumption is a fallacy. The snowfall rates after the Flood were prodigious. Tremendous thicknesses of ice were produced in a short time. The secular worldview does not accept catastrophic snow depositions and glacial buildups. Furthermore, variations in depositions due to storms and warm periods together with variations in dust accumulations, such as volcanic dust, would produce layering that would not be valid indications of years but rather cycles within one year. (A large storm with dust can produce the appearance of an annual layer.) In summary, the worldview of the interpreter will probably determine both the analysis and the interpretation.

Ice core dating is a new discipline. Its measurements require considerably more research, especially by those who do not hold secular assumptions.

Stria of the Southern Ice Mass

In proving that Pangaea divided during the Glacial Epoch, one aspect of that proof are the directions and dating of the stria produced by the Southern Ice Mass. To determine the directions and dating in South America, Africa, India, and Australia, we need to analyze the uncovered stria. Concerning covered stria, we need to establish that the debris or sediments covering that stria are not "old," making the stria "old," but are Pleistocene and contemporaneous with, or younger than the stria. (Concerning this issue, see footnotes 4, 9 and 11 of Chapter 13.) A thorough examination of the uncovered and covered stria should establish the thesis of this book – that all continental (not mountain) stria of the southern hemisphere were produced by the "Pleistocene" Glacial Epoch and not by a supposed "Paleozoic" Glacial Epoch. The evidence will prove that this stria was produced by the Southern Ice Mass *before* Pangaea divided.

Further Research Footnotes:

1 - Electric conductivity in melts create magnetic fields. Nature, May 27, 2004, 356, 399.

2 - Oxygen has three isotopic forms, two of which are used in seeking to determine past climatic conditions. They are ^{16}O and ^{18}O. The numbers express their relative weights. ^{16}O is by far the most abundant isotope (99.76%). The average ratio of ^{18}O to ^{16}O is 0.2%. The most mobile form, the oxygen in the water that evaporates more readily is ^{16}O, the lighter oxygen. Which isotope dominates in a snowfall is determined by the temperature of that atmosphere. By establishing the ratio of ^{18}O to ^{16}O in a layer of glacial ice with respect to the normal atmospheric ratio, the temperatures of the past atmospheres can sometimes be determined. Nature, Sept 1, 2005, 39.

BIBLIOGRAPHY

Books
- Ackerman, P.D., It's a Young World AfterAll, Baker Book House, Grand Rapids, MI, © 1986
- Antevs, E., The Recession of The Last Ice Sheet in New England, American Geographical Society Research Series, No. 11, New York, © 1922
- Austin, S.A., Ed., Grand Canyon, Monument to Catastrophe, Institute for Creation Research, Santee, CA, © 1994
- Biblical Archaeology Review, Washington DC
- Charlesworth, J.K., The Quaternary Era, Vol. 1 & 2, Edward Arnold Publ., London, © 1957
- Chernicoff, S. & Whitney, D., Geology, 3rd Ed. Houghton Mifflin Co. Boston, © 2002
- Coffin, H.G., Brown, R.H., Gibson, L.J., Origin By Design, Review & Herald Publishing, Hagerstown, MD.
- Creation Science Fellowship, The Proceedings of the Second [1990], And the Fifth [2003] International Conferences of Creationism [ICC], Pittsburgh, PA
- Encyclopaedia Britannica Inc., Chicago
- Faulkner, D. Universe by Design, Master Books, Green Forest, AR © 2004
- Flint, R.F., Glacial Geology & the Pleistocene Epoch, Wiley, New York, © 1947
- Hamblin, W.K. & Christiansen, E.H., Earth's Dynamic Systems, 9th Ed., Prentice Hall, NJ, © 2001
- Humphreys, D.R., Starlight and Time, Master Books, Colorado Springs, CO, © 1994
- Longwell, C.R., Knopf, A. & Flint, R.F., Physical Geology, 3rd Ed., Wiley, New York, © 1948,
- Lutgens, F.K. & Tarbuck, E.J., Foundations of Earth Science, 3rd Ed., Prentice Hall, NJ, © 2003
- Morris, H.M. & Whitcomb, J.C., The Genesis Flood, Presbyterian & Reformed Publishing Co., Philadelphia, PA, © 1963
- Morris, H.M., Scientific Creationism, Master Books, Green Forest, AR, © 1996
- Mulfinger, G. Jr., Design and Origins in Astronomy, Creation Research Society Books
- Ollier, C. & Pain, C., The Origin of Mountains, Routledge, London, © 2000
- Plummer, C.C., McGeary, D. & Carlson, D.H., Physical Geology, 10th Ed. McGraw-Hill, New York, © 2005
- Ramaswamy, S., The Lost Land of Lemuria, University of California Press, Berkeley, CA, © 2004
- Thompson, G.R. & Turk, J., Modern Physical Geology, 2nd Ed. Harcourt Brace & Co. ©1997
- Vardiman, L., Sea-Floor Sediments and the Age of the Earth, © 1996. Climates Before & After the Genesis Flood: Numerical Models and Their Implications © 2001, Institute For Creation Research Technical Monographs, El Cajon, CA.
- Von Engeln, O.D. & Caster, K.E., Geology, McGraw-Hill, New York, © 1952
- Williams, A. & Hartnett, J., Dismantling the Big Bang, Green Forest, AR, © 2005

Periodicals
- Biblical Archaeology Review, Washington, DC
- Creation Research Society Quarterly, Chino Valley, AZ,
- Nature, Nature Publishing Group, London
- Science News, Washington, DC
- Science, American Association For the Advancement of Science, New York, NY
- Scientific American, New York, NY
- Technical Journal, Acacia Ridge D.C., Australia

CREDITS

INDEX – PEOPLE

INDEX – PLACES

INDEX – SUBJECTS continued